Wakefield Press

Lost in Laos

Lydia Laube never says no to adventure, whether that means galloping a horse across the Mongolian plains or hopping on a cargo ship to Madagascar. Born into the farming community of Caltowie in the mid-north of South Australia, Lydia trained as a nurse in Adelaide, then set off to see the world. Her debut book, *Behind the Veil: An Australian nurse in Saudi Arabia*, was an instant bestseller, and she has become one of Australia's favourite travel writers. *Lost in Laos* is her eighth book. Between winter escapes to the sun, Lydia shares a small house in Adelaide with a large cat with attitude.

Also by Lydia Laube

Behind the Veil
Bound for Vietnam
Is this the Way to Madagascar?
Llama for Lunch
Slow Boat to Mongolia
Temples and Tuk Tuks
The Long Way Home

Lost in Laos

LYDIA LAUBE

**Wakefield
Press**

Wakefield Press
1 The Parade West
Kent Town
South Australia 5067
www.wakefieldpress.com.au

First published 2010

Cover design by Dean Lahn, Lahn Stafford Design
Typeset by Clinton Ellicott, Wakefield Press
Printed in Australia by Griffin Press, Adelaide

National Library of Australia Cataloguing-in-Publication entry

Author: Laube, Lydia, 1948–   .
Title: Lost in Laos/Lydia Laube.
ISBN: 978 1 86254 926 5 (pbk.).
Subjects:
Laube, Lydia, 1948–   – Travel – Laos.
Laos – Description and travel.
Dewey Number: 959.4

Government
of South Australia

Arts SA

fox creek
wines

Contents

1 Land of a Million Elephants

Land of a Million Elephants! How could anyone resist a place with a name like that?

A scan of the map of South-East Asia revealed that Laos, the country that formerly gave itself such an intriguing title, was the only place I hadn't visited. This had to be rectified. Over the years I had watched Laos progress through war, unrest and upheaval until it was relatively settled. In 1989 the Lao government relaxed enough to permit tourism, but it was controlled and restricted, making it difficult to get about. Finally, individual travel was possible. Right, I decided, now Laos is ready for me – I am off!

But of course I couldn't go straight there like any sane, sensible person. Laos is a landlocked country of 236,800 square kilometres. It shares borders with Cambodia, China, Burma, Thailand and Vietnam, so adventures could be had along the way if I travelled there overland after flying to Singapore. Excellent trains run from Singapore up the Malaysian Peninsula, into Thailand and across to Laos. I had fond memories of the train journey I had taken from Singapore to Bangkok back in 1970 when I had first set off to see the world and I thought it would be great to do it again. On that trip I had followed the regular tourist route up the west coast, but studying the map now I saw that there is an alternate way. Branching off from Kuala Lumpur is another train line known as the 'Jungle Line'.

Little used except by local people, it crosses the Malaysian Peninsula and terminates on the east coast close to the Thai/Malaysian border.

I got off to a fairly bad start – well, I was not even started when, attempting to collect my US dollar travelling cash from the Travelex office at Adelaide Airport, I discovered that I had not, as I thought, already paid for them. (I had been so proud of myself for managing this twenty-first century achievement on the internet, but pride, as I have often been reminded, goes before a fall.) Next I found that I had left my number one credit card – the one with money in it with which I was about to rectify this deficiency – in my other handbag, the one that was right then sitting at home in my wardrobe. How could I have done such a stupid thing? Easily, was the obvious answer. Maybe I am getting past being allowed out on my own. I paid for the dollars with card number two, my back-up card, in which there was no money, only credit.

I had plenty of time to consider the dilemma of how to transfer some funds into card number two when the next hiccup appeared. The plane was declared to be two hours late due to some bother it had encountered in Sydney. I had a deadline of nine pm to meet in Singapore. That was the time my train ticket would be held for me to collect. (in another major triumph on the internet I had established an almost pen pal relationship with a wonderfully helpful woman at Malaysian Rail, who, over a number of emails, had chatted me through the intricacies of the ticketing system.)

Idly flipping through the little red notebook that has accompanied me on many adventures, I noticed the express line phone number for my bank account. I had completely forgotten about that since I had taken up with the internet.

I phoned the number and managed to locate a real person instead of the usual machine and she, bless her, transferred a slab of cash into card number two for me. Problem solved.

Meanwhile Qantas, in its infinite generosity, compensated the delayed passengers languishing in the airport with ten dollars worth of sustenance from the kiosk in the departure lounge. Airport prices ensured that this did not allow for much expansion into high living. Poor payment for two hours in departure mode. I wondered whether a certain nameless Qantas CEO would be happy with a sandwich and a small black coffee for two hours of his time. But I have become philosophical about delays in travelling and always come prepared. No longer allowed to indulge in the highly suspicious practice of knitting, now I carry a book in my handbag. I also found some Singaporean students from Adelaide University to talk to. They told me that it was holiday time and they, along with many other students, were on their way home for the break.

Finally airborne, the plane made up some time and we arrived in Singapore only an hour late. Entry formalities were swift. I sprinted straight through immigration and into a taxi that sped me to the train station, a twenty-minute drive away. By then it was almost nine. I'd had the sense to pick up some Singapore dollars along with my US cash in Adelaide Airport and this saved some time. The exchange rate had been good at 1.25 to the Australian dollar. The ticket seller at the train station wasn't my nice friend of the internet chats; he grumpily demanded to know why I hadn't collected my ticket before this. But he gave it to me anyway.

I had pre-booked a room at the Royal Peacock Hotel in Chinatown. At $105 it was one of the cheapest I could find apart from the backpacker hostels that were all too far from the railway station for an early morning exit. I find

Singapore pretty expensive these days. As the taxi weaved and threaded its way through the tiny, crowded streets of Chinatown, the driver dropped dark hints about this location's respectability, or lack thereof. The Royal Peacock is one of the old Chinese shop-houses, many of which were former brothels that have been sanitised and born again as small hotels. As I waited for attention at its front desk in the cramped foyer, I suspected that the Royal Peacock might not have quite made the transition to absolute decorum. Some of its previous infamy appeared to linger; a man beside me was negotiating a price for a stay of a couple of hours.

Finally turning her unenthusiastic attention to me, the receptionist gave me an off-hand greeting and waved me in the vague direction of the lift. I dragged my bag to my closet of a room, so dark I couldn't see into the cupboards or my bag when I opened it on the bed. Dingy and in bad repair, nothing in that room worked – all the switches and knobs were broken or seized in one position, including those of the air-conditioner, which were set firmly on freezing and couldn't be turned down. Worse, the operation of the shower was complicated and it produced just a trickle of hot water. I was not amused.

I slept poorly. If I turned off the air-conditioner I suffocated, but with it on I froze. I gave up and got up at five am, which was a good thing as the wake-up call I had ordered didn't come. I had also arranged a taxi at reception the night before. This was a mistake. The same type of taxi that had made the trip from the train station for four dollars the night before had now metamorphosed into the Hotel Limousine and cost five times as much to return there.

But at last I was at the grand old Singapore Railway Station in Keppel Road. I love this wonderful colonial art deco remnant. Built by the Malaysian Transport Authority in 1932 on land leased for 999 years from the Singaporean government, it is huge, lofty and spacious. I entered the station's vast central waiting hall with its soaring domed roof and large windows that give it a splendid feeling of openness and light. The walls between the windows are hung with large painted pictures of Malaysian life – workers planting rice, tapping rubber trees, mining tin and driving bullock carts. These panels and the floor blocks are made of a particular type of rubber that deadens noise, adding to the feeling of calm in the hall.

Rows of seats line the sides of the waiting hall, but there was still plenty of open space to glide my bag across the smooth floor. I had no problem finding my way around. At the end of the hall are two large signs, Arrivals and Departures, and the train lines, covered by umbrella-shaped concrete roofs, proceed out or in from there. But first I gravitated to the food court on one side of the hall. At one stall I watched a local breakfast specialty being made. As a thin, flat pancake was cooking on a hot griddle, an egg was broken over it, then topped with a slice of cheese. I bought two. I was ravenous. Arriving too late for a meal at the hotel the night before, I'd had no further chance of food since the meagre rations I'd received on the plane. I thoroughly enjoyed my breakfast, and washed it down with a mug of strong black coffee to jump-start the day.

Afterwards I waited on a bench beside the departure sign until a pair of metal grilled doors clanged open, my ticket was checked, and I was allowed to advance to my seat on the train.

Soon we were on our way. The passenger seated beside me was an interesting British woman. She told me that she now lived in Switzerland where she worked for a pharmaceutical company doing research on malarial prophylactics, mainly Artemis, a product derived from the wormwood plant. I found this fascinating. Combating the ever-lurking malarial bugs when travelling is a burden I can do without.

It doesn't take long to cross the island of Singapore; its total land mass is only 581 square kilometres. From the Keppel Street train station on the far side of the island we soon arrived at the Johor–Singapore Causeway that leads to Malaysia. The causeway, which is roughly a kilometre long, was opened in 1923. Before the causeway connecting the island to the mainland was built, passengers and goods came across the island on a local train, were conveyed by ferry to the Malaysian Peninsula and then transferred onto a Malaysian train. Now border formalities are completed at Tanjong Pagar, on the end of Singapore Island, and the train rumbles onto the causeway and proceeds into Malaysia. Sadly, the crossing of the causeway did not delight me the way it had when first I had come this way. Then, travelling over water in a train to reach another country had been a new and exciting experience for a novice traveller. I'd had a sleeping compartment in a terrific old British train with wood panelling and little table lamps with fringed shades. I still have vivid memories of the bright blue sea that had sparkled on either side of the train on the narrow causeway. But now, heavy traffic on the road that ran beside the train line almost occluded the sight of the sea, and this day the sky was overcast and what water I could see was dull and grey.

Once we reached Malaysia, however, I cheered up, pleasantly surprised that large tracts of the country still appeared untouched. There were masses of vegetation, mainly palms, and lots of water in the form of streams and ponds. After poor, parched Australia's long, dry drought, this utterly green world was breathtaking; wall-to-wall and floor-to-ceiling luxurious emerald and jade, it rolled away as far as I could see.

After a while the train's dining car opened for business and I smartly lined up to offer my custom. Although the rest of this train was modern and the cafeteria car was gaily decked out with bright blue tables and red plastic seats, it was not air-conditioned. Lingering was not an option – the cooking was done in situ, in a cubbyhole behind the counter. Meals were limited to either a rice or a noodle dish. I had both, but for decency's sake and in an attempt to disguise my gluttony I waited an hour between them. I also tried for coffee but failed. Coffee came pre-packaged and heavily sugared. It could not be separated. Whatever do diabetics do in this country? I got funny looks when I asked for 'tidak gulas' or 'sensa manis' – no sugar or not sweet.

The train was comfortable and the journey was pleasant enough, but it seemed to last a lot longer than the eight hours it did take. Even though it had been described as an express, this train stopped frequently and we were an hour late into Kuala Lumpur. The conductor, a cheerful young Malaysian man, told me along the way that the problem was with the train. I asked, 'Is it sakit – sick?' He laughed and said, 'Yes, that is why we go slower.'

The new Kuala Lumpur train station is rather like a miniature Changi Airport, three massive floors with shops and stalls galore. I did a couple of circuits of most of it before I located the booking office where I had been told to collect the ticket I had reserved via the internet. I was taking the train from Kuala Lumpur that travels the Jungle Line, traversing the peninsula and heading for the east coast. I intended to get off at Wakif Bharu, the nearest station to the Thai border, from where I could cross into Thailand and get a train to Bangkok.

The staff at the ticket office had trouble finding my booking. Punching my name into the computer did not work until I realised that the ticket might have been lodged under any combination of my three names – my family name not necessarily being obvious to a Malaysian. Suggesting that it could be listed under my first name, I left them to it and wandered off to change some money.

2 In training

When I came back my ticket had materialised and I was delighted to find that costs in Malaysia were refreshingly inexpensive after Singapore's excesses. My first-class sleeper on the Malaysian train had cost a pittance.

Dropping my bag at the left luggage office, I went exploring and came upon the VIP lounge. Here, those exalted members of society who possess a first-class ticket can rest and refresh themselves in comfort. At last I had made it to VIP status! I was certainly not passing up this opportunity. Installing myself on a plush couch in a huge room that came complete with showers and a giant TV screen, I wallowed in opulence. After a wash and a rest I played with my little travelling computer, inserting its plug adapter into the TV's wall socket to connect it. This was more than the station staff had bothered to do. Rather than spend a couple of dollars on an adaptor for the super-duper TV's plug, someone had merely bent its prongs and forced them into the slots. Nice.

Later, on the prowl for nourishment again, I located an immense food hall. Circulating around the numerous stalls I chose a meal by the 'look and point' method. Rows of taps and basins for hand-washing lined both walls of the hall. What a good idea. We should do this in Australia. Although it is more necessary in Malaysia, where it is accepted practice to use your fingers to eat with instead of cutlery. A naturally messy eater, I would like to see this custom universally adopted. It would save a lot of shirt cleaning and washing up.

Then it was on to investigate the shops, among which were several big shoe outlets sporting a great selection of sandals. I found several pairs that I would have liked to buy but they were all too wide for my skinny feet. But I did splash out and, for the princely sum of one Malaysian dollar (three to an Australian), became the proud owner of a terrifically gaudy hair clip.

At eight in the evening my train was announced and I made an easy departure. Riding down an escalator, I skimmed along the smooth platform and hopped into the carriage where my admirable cabin awaited. The bed had been made up ready for me, with crisp white sheets, a blanket and a pillow with a snowy cover on which two cellophanewrapped choccie biscuits nested. There was a hand basin on the wall, on the rim of which two bottles of drinking water stood – as a warning against drinking from the tap I presumed – a chair, a small pull-down table, a bin and, oh what a blessing, air-conditioning that I could turn down.

I woke at five am when the train stopped for a long time at a station, and I didn't sleep again. It was dawn and now I could see the country we were traversing. It contained large areas of wilderness, interspersed with an occasional rubber plantation and now and then great patches of land that had been stripped – the red earth showing through like raw wounds – ready for palms to be planted for palm oil production.

The countryside appeared sparsely populated. Some of the small train stations we passed through were abandoned and derelict, the buildings and houses only shells; holes in their walls where windows had once been were now sightless eyes that watched the jungle encroaching. Trains no longer stopped at these stations, the railway had lost its transport dominance to the newly built road. But there is hope that the railway may soon regenerate. A new service meant to attract tourists along this route is planned.

Where inhabited houses or huts backed onto the railway line their most noticeable feature was the awful amount of rubbish that accompanied them – they were awash with refuse that simply had been chucked out of their back doors. But even among this litter the attendant vegetation grew lushly enough to soften its revulsion and create a kind of beauty. One rustic place's rear end was overhung by a falling-down pole and tin verandah made utterly gorgeous by a mantle of white, pink and green bougainvillea flowers that stood a metre high above it and cascaded to the ground like a floral waterfall, glorifying its humble construction.

The information I had obtained from the internet about the train I was on had declared that it had no food car and was scheduled to arrive at Wakif Bharu at nine-thirty in the morning. Feeling that I could survive until then I had brought no emergency vittles, but this supposed advent time came and went and by eleven I was flagging. Apparently work on the line had slowed our progress and we were running very late.

In the corridor I met an old gentleman from the next compartment. I asked him how long it would be before we arrived at Wakif Bharu. The stations that had come and gone had not been announced and I had no idea where I was. After the initial welcome of the previous evening, I had seen no train staff. Now I learned that there had not only been a food car open for business at breakfast time, but a trolley had been wheeled around with edible offerings. I had missed it all. Not something I usually do.

The old gentleman also told me that I should get off at Mas rather than Wakif Bharu, the town the internet information had advised. He said that Mas was a bigger town and closer to the border, so transport was easier to find than in Wakif Bharu. My new friend, Mr Habib, told me that his father had been a local stationmaster and the family had lived in a series of station houses in this location during his youth. I decided that he was a better bet than the internet, whose advice so far had not impressed me. It had cost me my breakfast! Not, in my opinion, a forgivable sin. I decided to abandon their dodgy counsel and follow Mr Habib's instructions.

Mr Habib also told me that the British had built this train line in the 1920s. It must have been quite a feat – the railway dipped and climbed, fording many deep gullies and rivers with bridges. Now retired, Mr Habib said that he had been a district officer under the British and later had worked in the same capacity for the Malaysian government. He had a daughter in Melbourne, a professor of medicine, who was married to an Australian. I asked him from where he was travelling and he said that he had been to Aceh to help rebuild mosques destroyed or damaged in the tsunami of 2004. Obviously a kind man, he gave me some tea from his thermos and a bottle of water to take with me – which later saved me from perishing of dehydration during the long wait I had for the Thai train.

At Mas Mr Habib helped me offload onto the platform and then hailed a nearby man offering transport. A smooth talker rushed up to head the first man off at the pass and, elbowing him away, shouted that he would take me to the border at Sungai Kolok for thirty Malaysian dollars. I didn't like this approach so I said firmly, 'I want this other man', to the elbowed one who stood back meekly. I had looked into his eyes and decided that he was the better man. He wore the white cap of a *hajji* and hopefully the pilgrimage to Mecca had made him virtuous, I thought, as he took off with my bag, leaving me to negotiate my way down to his car from the opposite end of the platform.

It was a twenty-minute drive to the border. The *hajji's* car was not in good nick; ominous rumblings came from its undercarriage, but we arrived safely. My driver took me as close as he could to where a four-lane highway, clogged solid with vehicles and whizzing motorbikes, passed through checkpoints and barriers. He indicated that this was as far as he could go and seemed to be offering to find a moto (motorbike transport) to take me further. My problem now was that since leaving Mr. Habib on the train I had not come across anyone who spoke English. And now they spoke Thai so my basic Malay was useless. I had been the only foreign tourist on the train; I had not seen another westerner after leaving KL.

A footpath beside the road led to a pedestrian entry to the Malaysian Immigration Office. I set off to walk through. Hiking past the line of cars and motorbikes waiting to go into the checkpoints in the roadway, I strolled through a gate and into immigration. Obtaining the necessary stamp in my passport to say that I had left Malaysia, I continued on, believing (mistakenly, I was later and most painfully to learn) that I had completed the transit into Thailand. Now I know that I should have hired a moto at the place where the taxi had left me and the rider would have taken me to Thai, as well as Malaysian, immigration, before ferrying me on to the train station. But walking further along the road after leaving Malaysian Immigration, I saw no sign indicating that I had to stop anywhere else. There was no barrier across the road – not even a hint – that I had, in fact, crossed over the border into Thailand.

I carried on, looking for the train station. On the opposite side of the road I noticed a hut-like building. I scanned it for signs of trains but nothing betrayed its function. A few people stood about its entrance but I was in train mode and, failing to twig that I needed this place for any reason whatsoever, I concluded that it was of no use to me and kept on moving. On reflection, I realised that this nondescript dump was actually the Thai Immigration Office. But there was no sign, no barricade and no one stopped me – I just toddled past it.

I asked several people where the train station was but no one understood me. Finally one man said 'moto', and pointed to one by the side of the road. I hopped on the back of the bike and the rider and I took off. The station was a few minutes ride away. Dismounting and crossing several train lines to reach the platform, I asked a uniformed guard if the train that stood on the line was going to Bangkok. It was, but it was not the express for which I had a ticket. I had bought my Thai train tickets via the internet but they could not be collected on arrival in the country like those of Singapore and Malaysia. They had to be paid for in advance and had been mailed to me. Fortunately I didn't get on this train. No English was spoken here, but when I presented my ticket to the guard, he shook his head, pointed at the clock and held up two fingers. I had two and a half hours to wait at Sungai Kolok station.

Investigating the possibilities of entertainment the platform might provide, I found a toilet with two attendants employed to collect six cents from me, possibly the only customer they had in the two hours I waited there. Their ablutions block was extremely clean; considering their lack of trade the two ladies had plenty of time to swab the place out. Further along, at an open-air food stall, I bought a glass of strong, aromatic coffee. A train policeman, clad in a well-fitting navy uniform and armed with a massive piece of weaponry the size of a small cannon, was tucking into his lunch at a nearby table. Two more patrolled the platform.

They posed smiling for me when I asked if I could photograph them.

As well as the train police, Sungai Kolok station also bristled with military personnel toting substantial defensive hardware. Insurrection and rebellion are rife in this part of southern Thailand. Terrorists killed two people here that week. Soldiers patrolled up and down the platform and a bunch of them travelled aboard each train as well as the train police. I wondered if this should reassure me or make me nervous. Looking at their heavy khaki uniforms I wondered how the soldiers coped in this gaspingly hot midday heat. It must be appallingly uncomfortable in all that clobber. They wore several different kinds of uniform and it took me a while to realise that one of the soldiers was a woman; decked out as she was in a most ungainly outfit, from bulky socks to a daggy big floppy hat, you couldn't tell.

Another train arrived and the guard signalled that I should board this one. I dropped my bag into my compartment. I had paid for the sole use of the cabin – not that this was expensive. Once more I was the only foreigner on the train, which, though not as superior as the Malaysian one, was perfectly adequate and quite comfortable. And I liked the loo at the end of the carriage. It was a spacious all-stainless steel squat model with handrails on each side wall and a hose with a squirter on the end in lieu of toilet paper. I couldn't see a familiar-looking flush button and I hesitated before the big red knob on the wall, remembering the debacle I had caused by mistaking a similar item on an Italian train and setting off a clamorous alarm bell. But finally, gritting my teeth, I pushed the button and, much to my relief, all it did was the flush the toilet.

The train left the station almost on time. Three blasts of the guard's whistle and a hoot of the train horn and we were off.

3 Thailand's most wanted

I was now in Thailand. The countryside looked much the same as Malaysia, but the difference that I couldn't fail to notice was the military presence. This was a little unnerving. Each station we passed through had at least six heavily armed soldiers patrolling the platform. More soldiers travelled on the train, touring up and down the length of it, while a train policeman was positioned at each end of every carriage. And they all seemed to be on the alert, not lounging about with the bored indifference of a routine presence.

The sight of so much armed force made me aware that the terrorists in this southern part of Thailand included attacking trains in their repertoire of mischief-making. I remained a little uneasy until finally, by the next morning, I saw no more soldiers on the stations. Instead there were monks sitting on platform seats and the gilded roofs of Buddhist temples shone among the palms. I saw no more mosques; Islam had given way to Buddhism.

This train did not run to a dining car, but soon after departure an attendant had brought along a menu from which I could order lunch, dinner or breakfast that would be home delivered. I went for it all. I had an estimated eighteen hours to put in on this journey. The total price for my eating spree came to the equivalent of a mere four-teen Australian dollars. In between feeding my face, I read and played with my computer. And of course inspected the country. The train stations were well kept, decorated with large ornamental pots containing trees and bushes, and surrounded by pleasant gardens with lots of bright greenery. I guess it's not hard to have luxuriant gardens and flowers when you have as much rain as they do.

Halfway through the night I woke and for some reason thought about my Thai visa. Then a horrible realisation hit me. I could not remember actually getting a visa. Thunderstruck I leapt out of the bunk to check my passport. It was true! I didn't have a visa. Hells bells! What had I done? Then I saw it clearly. The Malaysian side of the border had a barrier that could not be passed without presenting your passport but the Thai side hadn't. This was not usual. Borders, in my experience, are always closed, iron-tight, against casual popping over. There is no way you can get through them without being checked. I had received Malaysian exit stamps and, not being halted at any other point, had blithely sailed on without realising that I had not visited the Thai office.

With the clarity of hindsight I now remembered the grotty hut beside the road on the way to the train station. Of course, though it was so unlike the smartly efficient Malaysian Immigration Office, it must have been the Thai one. I had noticed people coming from the other direction going in there, but I was the only traveller approaching from the Malaysian side. It hadn't registered with my food-depleted brain. I had only been looking for a train station. Oh boy was I in trouble!

My train arrived in Bangkok two hours late at half-past eleven that morning. I went immediately to the Tourist Information desk in the station and explained my visaless state. But this was Sunday! All visa offices were shut. The helpful staff tried to call the Tourist Police. They didn't work on Sundays either. Tourists should be going to church and not out getting into trouble on Sundays! I knew that Bangkok, rather than a remote border outpost, would be a better location in which to fix this problem, but my train ticket was paid for. I had to go on. After all, I hadn't done anything wrong, right? Wrong! I was to regret this decision.

I had nine hours to wait until my train left that evening. I dropped my bag at the left luggage office, but Bangkok station had no posh waiting room like that of Kuala Lumpur. It was just a matter of hanging around in the extremely large waiting hall. But what a hall it was, like a huge, domed plane hangar. Approaching the station from the platform, you are confronted by a gigantic portrait of the Thai king, Bhumibol. Inside, another picture of the king flanked by one of the queen, Sirikit, dominates the hall. Large numbers of people filled this place. They sat in groups on the terrazzo floor or on the rows of red plastic chairs that lined the sides. Now and then there would be a flurry of movement as the imminent departure of a train was announced, but the crowd never seemed to diminish.

A mezzanine floor ran along both upper sides of the hall. On this was a coffee house and a restaurant as well as more seating. The food court was downstairs, off to one side. Here you acquired food by purchasing vouchers from a booth and exchanging them for whatever you fancied among the offerings of the stalls that lined the sides of the court. You then ate at one of the tables in the middle of the big room. The food sat in open bowls on waist-high counters in front of the stalls, not an overly hygienic arrangement, but it all looked interesting. I patrolled the place until I decided what I wanted, then bought a fistful of coupons and went on a spree. I selected steamed chicken cut up on a pile of rice and topped this with a wonderful sauce of chilli, garlic and lime juice from a lineup of condiments. Then I went to another stall and bought a bottle of water and a mug of great, strong local coffee. All this princely fare cost $1.80.

Then it was time to inspect the bathroom facilities. Two attendants, as well as two turnstiles, guarded the entrance in case you try to slip in without forking over the required two baht. (Currently there were thirty-two baht to one dollar Australian.) The toilet block's spacious interior was maintained in a spotless state by a cleaner, busy all the time wielding mop and bucket.

Time passed. I could have wandered out and surveyed the surrounding streets but I couldn't summon the enthusiasm. Bangkok is not new to me. I have been there several times in the past. Instead I investigated all the small shops and stalls that surrounded the sides of the hall. The book-shop prices were cheap, the latest novels all about ten dollars. Then there were snacks, donuts, chips and ice-cream. I passed on these and opted for a foot treatment in the massage parlour – an hour of relaxation was what I needed.

Afterwards I moved upstairs to the mezzanine floor where I sat reading for a couple of hours on the wooden seats that overlook the ground floor. A visit to the coffee shop occupied more time. The coffee was express and good and cost the same as my entire lunch in the less trendy food court downstairs.

At six pm, as happens every day, loudspeakers began to play the national anthem and the crowd leapt to their feet to stand reverently at attention. I joined them. Thais have enormous respect for their beloved king and I had no wish to offend local sensibilities in any way. I have heard that this can prove unwise.

I had dinner at the mezzanine restaurant – Anna's Place. The fish steak I ordered came smothered in mayonnaise and the entire edge of the plate was also covered with artistic squirts and swirls of this bright-yellow goo. I never saw so much mayonnaise! I am not a fan of this stuff; I wiped off what I could and asked for some chilli. The fish, when I eventually got through to it, was excellent.

Finally it was time to collect my bag and head for the platform where my train stood waiting. I boarded unassisted. No one checked me on, took my ticket, or even looked at me. Just as well I knew my way around Thai trains by this time. The train was the same as the last one I had been on and I even had the same compartment number. A jolly, if huge and lumbering, quartet of young Irishmen took up residence in the compartments on either side of me. They were the first foreigners I had encountered since the Singapore–Kuala Lumpur train.

By now I was desperate for bed so when we left, almost on time, only a few minutes after half past eight, I hit the sack. An attendant then arrived to offer me dinner. I declined this but ordered breakfast for the following morning.

I woke at five am and, after the breakfast that had been delivered to my cabin, I was ready for departure at Nong Khai, on the border of Laos by eight, our supposed arrival time. Instead we arrived at eleven.

I climbed into a tuk tuk with a couple of young men, one Australian and one Swiss, and we sped to the border crossing. Then the fun started. I filled out the form provided, but when I fronted with it to the checkpoint I was refused entry and sent to the office on one side of the road. At least it was air-conditioned in there, as it was very hot and stickily humid outside. I tried to explain my situation – with very little success. I was viewed with dark suspicion, as though this had never happened before, a foreigner arriving without a visa. It took me a while to realise that the officials thought that I had been refused entry at the previous border crossing and had sneaked in anyway. Oh dear, this was not going to be considered an innocent mistake. Communication was limited. I have no Thai and they had little English. But one immigration officer did manage to convey the unwelcome fact to me that this was a very serious matter. I asked if I could pay a fine for this violation (they could construe this however they liked, a bribe or otherwise) but I was told it was not up to immigration to decide this affair. This was a police matter.

'OK,' I said, 'bring on the police.' I thought I could pay the police a fine and get off with a warning. 'No,' the officer said. 'This is for the court.'

This was not looking good! To get to court in Thailand can take months. And in the meantime I would have to stay in custody – a nice way of describing the Bangkok Hilton, Thailand's infamous gaol. I could not go to a hotel; I was not officially in the country. I had been declared an illegal immigrant!

'You wait,' the officer told me. I waited. Half an hour later I went through the entire production again with another man. He also said, 'You wait.' And again I waited. The next man to hear my story appeared to believe that I was merely stupid, not criminal. After two hours he said, 'I will take you to the border.' I voiced an opinion along the lines that he was only trying to get rid of me. 'If you have trouble they can call me,' he said. Oh yeah! The Thais and Lao barely speak to each other.

However, it was worth a try. An official immigration department dual cab utility arrived at the door. A big cellophane-wrapped gift basket of fruit was unloaded from the back seat to make room for me. As my escort came toward me with it I said, 'Oh, for me?' It always helps to make 'em laugh! My bag was hefted into the back and three uniformed officers got in with me. Force of numbers in case I tried to escape?

We drove across the Friendship Bridge that connects the two countries, but I wasn't in the mood for admiring the scenery as we crossed the wide Mekong River. One thing I couldn't miss though was a large, rather quaint sign as you approach Lao Immigration from the Thai side. It stated: 'Crossing the border to gamble is dangerous and the Thai government has no authority to help you.' And in clear view from here, over on the Lao side, looming above all around it, sat a huge square building with 'Slot Machine Gamble' written on it. No gambling in Thailand, while in Laos apparently it exists, but is not safe.

Dumped at the checkpoint on the Lao side, I filled out the form and joined the queue. Surprise, surprise, I was rejected. This time no discussion would even be entered into. A severe woman spoke to me through a tiny window in a big room. 'No.' she said, 'No Thai exit visa, you go back.'

While I had been standing waiting in the queue, I had talked to an American, his Thai wife and a Lao man who now lived in Canada. They asked about my problem and very kindly tried to help me. When I was refused entry the Lao man did not give up on me but said he would try to speak to someone. He did this and was referred to the man in charge. I was dragged before this person to explain my sins and negligences, but even he couldn't help. Without an exit visa I could not come in. I still had to go back. Wondering what it would be like to live here in no man's land forever between two countries, I said a sad farewell to my supporters and champion, bought a ticket for the shuttle bus, and headed back over the river. At least I didn't have to walk the couple of kilometres.

Back at the Thai checkpoint, feeling like a boomerang, I was lumping my bag toward the office again when I encountered an official who asked where I was going. By an unbelievable piece of serendipity this man was the deputy head of the Immigration Department, on a visit to the border posts. Much bedecked with badges, medals and gold braid, he was not only important but a genteel, softly-spoken, fluent English speaker. Thank heaven he seemed to understand what I had done – that it was only a mistake and I had not committed a deliberate felony. With a charming smile, he gave me a glass of cold water and said, 'Wait.' (I seem to have heard that before!)

After some time he returned and told me that he could give me an exit stamp. Apparently he had contacted Sungai Kolok, the border crossing where all this had begun. (And that's a name I never want to hear again. I must have said it a thousand times that day.) Another fun-filled hour sitting anxiously in the office passed before the deed was done and my passport appeared with an entry visa and an exit stamp. I had to sign about twenty-five papers, copies of my train ticket, passport and various statements absolving all concerned of any blame. By this time I was ready to sign away my worldly goods to get out of there. The Thai visa was marked 'entry Sungai Kolok' and the exit, Nong Khai, where I was languishing at present. (I had, for what it was worth, crossed the entire country of Thailand and spent two days there without officially having entered!) I was never more relieved to get anything than that visa and I went on my way rejoicing, clutching it passionately.

I rattled back to the Laos border post on the shuttle bus and this time there were no problems. The attendants outside the office, who had been told my sad tale by my Lao friend, cheered me on my way. After all this hullabaloo the Lao visa was at least something to show for the trouble

I had endured to achieve it. It was a most elaborate and impressive article: large, multi-coloured and embellished with a gleaming silver medallion.

4 Laos at last

Finally on Lao soil, my first impression of the country known formerly as Land of a Million Elephants – White Parasol – was that it was more prosperous than I had imagined. From the border I took a taxi to the city of Vientiane. Five hours of stress had left me unfit to handle twenty-five kilometres in a crowded tuk tuk. However, my troubles were not over yet. By now I would have considered being mugged a minor hitch after the day I had just endured. My problem at this moment only involved finding a bed for the night.

The first hotel I tramped wearily into did not have a vacancy; neither did the second, the Beau Rivage, a small hotel on the Mekong waterfront. Its manager demanded a deposit to keep a room for me the next day. In my weakened state I forked over the ready, but later wished I hadn't as the guesthouse he sent me a short way up the road to – well, he called it a road but it was actually a potholed mud track – was very nice and much cheaper. There, at the Nalanthne Guesthouse, a smiling young man said he would be happy to accommodate me. I was so relieved I almost hugged him

The room was terrific. On the second floor, it faced the Mekong River and had a balcony overlooking the water. The Nalanthne was almost new, squeaky clean and equipped with everything I could possibly need. There was even satellite TV from which in the morning I got an Australian news channel. The building was tall and skinny and rows of little white theatre-box balconies decorated its façade, reminiscent of the small wedding cake hotels I had liked in Vietnam.

After a quick scrub up, my next priority was food. I'd had nothing to eat since seven that morning, a state of affairs rare for me but about to be rectified. The Nalanthne's restaurant, which gave guests a ten percent discount, was a couple of steps over the dirt track on the extreme edge of the river. Alarm bells should have rung at the sight of all those big trees and greenery alongside all that water, but before it registered I had already been bitten badly by sandflies – a tropical menace only one step less evil than fleas. I had put a little repellent on my feet but my hands and arms fell prey to these monsters and the next day I would be covered with big red swellings exuding fluid from their centres. Even my face was bitten. I was embarrassed to be seen. I looked like a plague victim. Someone should have been walking in front of me with a red flag and a bell calling, Unclean! Unclean!

But at the time I was interested only in food. To my joy, it was impressive and dirt cheap. Lao cuisine relies heavily on chilli, tamarind, coconut, fish paste and crushed peanuts, and is very tasty. I had a green papaya salad, a chicken dish and a coconut to drink. All this cost a couple of dollars. Beerlao, the excellent local beer, was a dollar a stubbie but red wine was on the menu so I asked to try it. The wine proved hard for the two staffers to find. There didn't seem to be much demand for it. The shelf behind the bar sported an imposing line up and I was offered the whisky and gin bottles before someone thought to look in the fridge. On its bottom shelf lay a cask of gut-rot red that had obviously been stagnating in there for quite a time. It tasted horrible.

To add insult to injury half a glass of this poisonous brew cost the same as my meal.

The local currency is the kip and the exchange rate was a whacking eight and a half thousand per US dollar, which is widely accepted in Laos, as is the Thai baht. I had come armed with cash amounts of both currencies. I soon learned that the amount of kip on a bill would be converted to whichever money you had, but as some hotels didn't give a good exchange rate it was best to get a stash of kip at a change office. Then you can pay with whatever currency you are asked for. I had to become accustomed to athletic leaps of mental arithmetic switching between dollars, baht and kip. Sums! Never my favorite occupation.

That night I was in bed by half-past seven and I slept for a long time. I had made it into Laos, now all I needed to do was recover. So far on this trip I had clocked up a swag of time with Murphy and I wondered when my stars were going to turn right way up again.

'Sabai di', good health, I was met with when I came downstairs the next morning. That and a big smile is the traditional Lao greeting – a good start to my restoration programme.

I would have been happy to remain in the Nalanthne Guesthouse, but I had given the Beau Rivage ten perfectly good dollars the night before so I packed my bag and had breakfast – 'blurred eggs' – which I'd never had before, nor am likely to again I imagine. Dragging my unwilling bag over the stones and potholes of the road/cart-track, I clattered the short distance to the Beau Rivage and checked in. Waiting for my room to be ready, I sat under the lovely trees beside the river and ordered tea. To my horror I was offered a tea bag and a mug of tepid water. This must be a tourist ghetto! I rectified the misconception that I preferred western trappings by telling the waiter that

I would like 'Lao tea', and this duly arrived in a pot in its natural state.

From where I sat I could see clearly across the river's wide expanse to the buildings of a town on the opposite bank. I had to remind myself that it was Thailand over there. Vientiane curves along a bend of the 1865 kilometres of the Mekong that form the border between Laos and Thailand. Watching a tree branch cruise swiftly by on the fast-flowing, muddy brown waters, I thought the pace of the river must be due to the current wet season influx. Later I was told that although its level is higher in the rainy season the river is always this colour and almost as speedy.

Establishing myself in the Beau Rivage, I declared this day Recovery Day, and all day didn't venture any further than to the riverbank to eat. The room I had been given was nice but it didn't face the river. As compensation, however, I had a magnificent tree. Even though this room was high on the second floor, the tree's branches encompassed the entire spread of the wall of glass that was the window. It had glossy dark-green leaves like that of a mango and bore a fig-like fruit that kept it constantly alive with the movement of birds, big and small, hopping about its branches.

Looking past the tree, on one side I could see the curved orange roof of a large temple, and on the other a backyard containing a brightly painted spirit house perched on a pole that each morning a woman came down to with offerings. Spirit houses had begun to appear not long after I had crossed into Thailand, when the mosques and the star and sickle moon of Malaysia's Islam had petered out.

My room had cable TV, but the set was positioned so far away in the high ceiling that I had to lie flat on the bed to see it. I had a play with all the channels and on the Chinese language channel I discovered that Kevin Rudd isn't the only Australian who speaks Mandarin. There was

Mel Gibson blathering away in it, courtesy of a dubbing arrangement.

I vegged out until food time when I walked back to the Nalanthne Guesthouse's restaurant. The fish I ordered came complete with head, tail, fins and eyes and had been fried to a crisp, but what I managed to chip off was delicious. Laos, I was rapidly discovering, is a pig's paradise. Then it was time for more sleep.

Breakfast in the Beau Rivage's restaurant was included in my room's price. It was the dread continental, but it came with a plate of delightfully arranged papaya, pineapple and dragon fruit, the speckled lovely I hadn't seen since Cambodia. And by paying an extra two dollars I obtained an excellent tomato and onion omelette. Now, Restoration Day over, I was ready to take on the town!

Ambling along the rutted track beside the river, I discovered that after a while it turned into a paved promenade that eventually became a pleasant corniche along the river's edge. On this strip I passed a money-changer, an internet office, small tour and travel businesses, but little traffic. Vientiane is the quietest capital city in South-East Asia and the slowest. Its sparse traffic still consists more of bicycle, tuk tuk and scooter than cars. Though Laos is on the move and much building is going on in Vientiane, it still has non-polluted air and a certain tranquility.

The weather this day was overcast, hot and sticky, but not unbearable. July is the rainy season and not the coolest time of the year but it is not the hottest either. I didn't find walking at this time of the day difficult. Turning away from the river towards the town centre, I hit one of the two main streets where I found more small shops and offices, as well as a bookshop that had an exchange option and little cafes offering all manner of food, including Indian and Thai.

Chanthaburi, City of the Moon, its sixteenth-century title, or 'Paris of the East', as it was known in its French heyday, Vientiane's name has always conjured up exotic visions. Today some of its former ambience remains. Keeping on past the commercial area, I found wide, tree-lined boulevards on which stood elegant French colonial buildings and ornate historic temples surrounded by towering palms and blossom-covered trees as well as the boxy, brutally plain Soviet Realist-style buildings of the communist era of the 1960s and 1970s.

Since its original settlement by southern Lao people in the 9th century, Vientiane's neighbours – Thailand, Vietnam and Burma – have all taken turns at occupying and controlling the city. In 1893 the French gained Laos as a colony and in the late 19th century they made Vientiane the capital, establishing a riverboat service that linked Laos to Cambodia and Vietnam, their other colonies. In 1949 the French granted Laos partial independence, but the Pathet Lao communist movement demanded full self-government and waged a long and intense resistance until full independence finally was achieved in 1953.

In 1961 the CIA formed a secret army in northern Laos in the hope of preventing the further spread of communism in Asia. In 1964, during the American aggression of Vietnam (to quote the local viewpoint), although Laos was nominally a neutral state it did lie between China and Vietnam. The USA began an assault against Lao ground targets they believed were providing support for the Viet Cong, and Laos became the most heavily bombed place in Asia. In nine years US planes dropped two million bombs – at a cost of two million dollars a day and a total cost of seven billion dollars – on Laos. Today a quantity of unexploded ordinance remains so care is needed when stepping off the beaten track. During this desperate time one-third of Lao's population of 2.1 million became external or internal refugees.

In 1975, after the fall of Vietnam, the Lao communist party seized power and established the Lao People's Democratic Republic. Abolishing the monarchy, they sent the king, queen and crown prince to a forced 'labour in the fields' imprisonment. No record exists of their fate but they did all die, possibly from malaria and malnutrition.

Now, after many years of insurgency and unrest, Laos has become relatively stable. A single-party socialist government with a considerably softened approach has replaced the initial severe communist regime.

5 Temples and tuk tuks

Heading back towards the river (I hoped), I stopped for sustenance at a cafe and ordered 'muesli with yogurt and fruit' from the menu. Sometimes menu items turn out to be not quite as expected. The yogurt was bright pink, there was no fruit and the muesli was an infinitesimal scatter of chaff. I talked to a young Lao woman who told me that she worked for a tour company. I said I was going next to check out a guesthouse I had read about called the Lani 1 with a view to staying there on my return to Vientiane. She asked, 'Can you ride a bike?' I replied, 'I hate bikes and the feeling is mutual.'

But then I discovered that she was asking whether if I could manage on the back of a motorbike. Perhaps she had thought I looked too delicate for this pursuit. I corrected this assumption, and, installing me on the back seat of her little moto, she very kindly drove me to the guesthouse.

The Lani 1 was located down a quiet leafy lane at the back of a massive temple complex. A fabulous old house, it had cool balconies, tranquil gardens and antique furniture. It was the same price as the Rivage, but although the position and the grounds were lovely, the rooms were too dark for my taste; I like a lot of light.

Back on the moto, Tina insisted on ferrying me further around town before leaving me back in the main street near the office of a company I wanted to ask about a riverboat trip. Here is a warning for the wise. Take note: at home on the internet I had read about river trips on this divine-looking boat, the *Vat Phou*, and if I had booked from there the price would have been horrendous, about five hundred dollars a day – two thousand in all. But in Laos I was quoted the local price and it was four hundred for the total four days, including the single supplement.

Next door to the tour place was an internet office and I spent a frustrating time trying to access my account. Vientiane has several of these small internet rooms that supply a service at around two dollars an hour. Noticing that the wee boy of the couple who ran the place was glued, highly amused, to something on the television in the corner, I sat down and joined him. Much more fun than Bigpond, he was watching Tom and Jerry on a local channel that plays cartoons by the hour. They are dubbed, so Tom and Jerry were speaking Thai, but you don't need to understand the language to appreciate them.

After a good dose of cartoons, I bought some bananas from a street stall – I think they must have been plantains, only used for cooking, as their green colour did not change and they never ripened – and returned to my room for some R and R.

Lying on the bed I decided that the tree was far better entertainment than the neck-breaking TV. The most amazing butterfly arrived to visit it. With a wingspan bigger than a sparrow's, this wonderful creature was patterned black and orange-yellow, like a tiger. Was this a tiger moth? Then a grey-brown bird perched on a branch and spread his white-edged tail like a peacock's fan. Beautiful.

After a shower and a rest it was time to gird the loins – cover myself with repellant – and brave the riverfront for food at my hotel's restaurant. It didn't help; I got even more sandfly bites. Every time I went near the river it was the same. Despite going to bed with an antihistamine tablet and hydrocortisone cream each night, I looked progressively more awful every day. I still had to go about looking mortifyingly like a pestilence victim or worse – a carrier.

For dinner that night I ate the Lao national dish, *laap* – minced and rolled balls of chicken, or it can be pork, or fish, mixed with herbs and green vegetables and served with lots of salad. The Beau Rivage's restaurant was tastefully decorated with much wood and open on three sides to the river breezes. As I sat eating I watched a great storm blow in from across the river. Rain poured down, turning the track outside to mud and the potholes into deep puddles. I sloshed back to my room. Since arriving in Laos my shoes had been a constant mess. No wonder 'no footwear inside' is the rule. Everywhere you go, you leave your shoes at the door.

I padded barefoot from the hotel front door to the reception desk, shoes in hand, to deposit them on my room's section of the wooden shelves there. After several hours of hard touristing, it was a blessed relief to get my shoes off and soothe my soles on the cool tiled floor.

Later I hailed a tuk tuk, planning to visit the Asian Pavilion Hotel made famous by John le Carré in his spy novel, *The Honourable Schoolboy*. In its previous life in the 1960s and 1970s, this hotel was called The Constellation and had been a notorious meeting place for all nationalities. After World War Two and during the Cold War, Vientiane had been known for foreign intrigue and general wickedness, and the Constellation was the hub of it all. But in 1975, when the war ended and communism arrived in Laos, all Vientiane's riotous living was over. More's the pity, I thought as with great expectations I entered the Asian Pavilion Hotel. A former haunt of spies and secret agents, this was a place that appealed to my romantic side. I was most disappointed to find it now very tame. No nefarious-looking types lurked in the foyer as I hiked across its large expanse of shiny floor; no infiltrator hid among the many fountains and potted plants. I reached the extensive polished wood reception desk and spoke to a young man who quoted me their prices – twenty dollars a single, or double for that matter. Checking their food supplies, I located the only restaurant the hotel now had. Beside the front entrance, it had tables on the footpath, cafe style, and only served western-style food.

Returning to the Rivage in a tuk tuk, the ruts in the riverside path seemed to have got worse since the night's rainstorm and the rattly little vehicle almost tipped over as we careered along, lurching and bouncing in and out of potholes. Tuk tuks are not very stable and I thought there was a good chance I might pitch onto the floor of this one. To compensate the poor driver for the wear and tear on his vehicle I arranged to hire him again in the morning. We agreed that he would come for me at ten and take me to the market.

Lao tuk tuks are similar to those found in neighboring countries – a motorbike with an attached container on two wheels behind for passengers. But so far the ones I had seen in Laos sat the passengers facing the rear, not like those of other places that face the front. Here they cost 20,000 kip to the town centre from the riverside and 30,000 to the market (around two to three dollars.) There are also jumbos which are bigger three-wheeled vehicles.

The next morning the staff in the Rivage's restaurant fed me breakfast again, fruit, coffee and omelette. I was the only customer but it took three smiling young men and the female cashier to look after my small needs. Promptly at ten, my tuk tuk driver arrived and announced himself to the staff. Putt-putting slowly along, looking out from the back of the tuk tuk, was a fine way to sightsee. We passed along the main avenue, said to be the Champs Élysées of Vientiane, a wide tree-lined boulevard containing the imposing white-walled presidential palace and Wat Si Saket, a massive, glittering, gold-studded temple complex.

Buddhism has been practiced in Laos since the thirteenth century and sixty percent of the population is Buddhist. The majority of the remainder are animists – spirit, or *phi*, worshippers – although many Buddhists observe respect for *phi* too. In the early days of communist rule Buddhism was repressed, but now it is tolerated. Although *phi* is supposedly forbidden, it also continues.

The tuk tuk dropped me at the entrance of Talat Sao, Vientiane's enormous general market. A vast indoor bazaar, it consists of two sections, the old and the new. The old is the original covered market – a great, green-roofed two-storied building, bursting, higgledy-piggledy, with activity. In front of it is the new – a modern air-conditioned mall with lots of small shops and stalls. Under awnings around the perimeter of the old market were shoemakers, goldsmiths and noodle soup stalls. Prices varied according to the position: at the back in the warm air of the old market, goods were cheaper.

There, with a lot of help from my friends – a nice young couple with a mobile phone stall – I bought and had installed a card for my phone. I was now, with considerable ease and very little expense, connected to Lao Telecom. Wow! How's that for a devout Luddite. I even used the phone to dial Luang Prabang, my next port of call, and book a room. The young woman at the phone stall, exclaiming over the horrible bites on my arms and face, took me by the hand and led me to a stall that sold all manner of interesting jars and bottles of potions and lotions. She and the owner examined me and, for a few cents, sold me a small bottle of oil that was remarkably effective in stopping the maddening itch I was suffering.

Next I bought a tiny pocket magnifier with a light for a couple of dollars. Then I found the gold shops. Gold, glorious gold, there was acres of it, in hundreds of tiny shops. It was a good price so I bought a necklace after much pleasant discussion (I prefer that term to bargaining.) The Lao are such polite and gentle people it's a delight to 'haggle' with them.

I loved this market. When the heat and humidity in the back blocks of the old market becomes too much, you can pop into the air-conned new part and retreat to the cafe for a meal and a sit down. There is even a decent toilet at one thousand kip a go. I spent hours happily fossicking around in both the old and new section. When I emerged it was raining again. I opted to walk back to the Rivage under my umbrella. It became cooler when it rained and then walking was enjoyable.

Following the road I had ridden along in the tuk tuk, I came to the rear entrance of the Lane Xang Hotel. Once the poshest hotel in town and a government showpiece, it had been built in the communist era – in the socialist square and ugly fashion – for the use of the party faithful, as opposed to the Constellation where the spies had hung out. Curious, I popped in for a look.

Through doors flashed open for me by smiling attendants, I swanned across its super grand lobby full of massive, elaborately carved wooden furniture. A single room, I was told at reception, cost thirty dollars. That may or may not be a bargain. I have learned over the years that the opulence of grand facades and lobbies of such establishments don't necessarily translate to the rooms upstairs.

The front entrance of the Lane Xang faces the river and coming out that way I passed a massage business. I had seen several enticing signs around the town offering massages and it seemed to be the thing to do, so I stopped. Perusing the list of prices, which were ludicrously low, I opted for the complete works – an aromatic oil, full-body job. The salon had a lovely ambience, low lights, flickering scented candles and small water fountains trickling softly. After a shower I had to remain completely naked. Although this was the first time I'd had to do the full monty for a massage, at least the operator was a woman. After a time she pointed to my face and told me I was very beautiful. When I asked her, 'What is beautiful?' it turned out to be my nose! Again! When the nurses in Saudi had told me this was what they thought admirable about me I had been completely floored. I would never have imagined that answer. My nose is the usual standard equipment. It fits my face and it works, which is about all that can be said for it, but apparently straight, thin noses are attractive to Asian eyes.

Later I was given a seat in the foyer and my masseuse brought me some herbal tea, offering the small flower-bedecked tray on her knees, the way that women make offerings to higher beings like monks. She then tied a piece of orange plaited thread around my wrist and recited a Buddhist prayer to restore my equilibrium. I trotted my restored equilibrium back along the riverbank to my room and rested it until teatime.

6 Don't eat the tofu

By evening I was ready to go walking again. This time I headed away from the riverside and its sandflies with their voracious appetites. Half an hour later I still had not come upon a restaurant. Then I saw a likely place, a couple of tables on the footpath in front of a shop. I stopped and indicated to the woman presiding over the cooking pot that I wanted to eat.

Groups of teenagers were drifting from a big building on the opposite side of the street. Three of them, two girls and a boy, crossed the road and asked if they could join me at my pavement table. The boy spoke a little English. He told me that the building was the 'higher school' and that he was studying economics. The girls were slim and pretty in their neat school uniforms – close-fitting, ankle-length navy-blue traditional wraparound skirts and white blouses. Lao faces seemed to me more like those of Burmese people than the Thai. They have fine features and many, even some of the boys, are downright gorgeous. I had read that the Lao are the most laid-back people in Asia, and so far the ones I had met verified this. I found them also to be kind and friendly.

A bowl of food was presented to me. It contained noodles among which floated unidentifiable pieces of flotsam and jetsam. Some might have been chicken. There were also large purplish chunks that by their texture I assumed were tofu flavoured with something or other. As I raised the last chunk of this on my chopsticks I asked the lad if it was tofu. 'No,' he said. 'Pig's blood.'

My now trembling hand continued its long, long journey to my reluctant mouth as I tried to ignore the screams of protest that came from my stomach. Rather than offend the witnesses, though, I put it in my mouth and forced myself to swallow. Was I taking aboard some foul disease? What I do for international relations!

Eventually the youngsters went on their way. I gathered that this place was the equivalent of the school's tuck shop. Its front was festooned with enticing racks of small packets containing biscuits and cakes. I investigated them all, hopeful of finding some peanuts, for which I had recently developed a craving. I had scoured the Talat Sao for them in vain.

Walking back towards the Mekong in the unlit darkness of the streets, I did not feel unsafe until I reached the inky gloom of the rutted track beside the river. The danger I feared, though, as I splashed and stumbled in and out of mud puddles, was not a lurking assassin but the great risk to which I was exposing my ankles.

The next day I had to get up at dawn, so it was an early night for me. Through negotiations with the Rivage's receptionist I had bought a bus ticket to Luang Prabang, the old Laotian capital in the north of the country – a nine-hour journey, all being well, from Vientiane.

The tuk tuk transport to the bus station that was included in the ticket price arrived at seven the next morning, but I still managed to shovel in some breakfast beforehand. In the restaurant I talked to a middle-aged Frenchman, who complained that Laos was now attracting too many shoe-string travellers who know nothing of the culture, have no regard for it and make no attempt to learn. He warned me to give one town a miss – Vang Vieng. Here, he said, these specimens are to be found in profusion, lying about tripped out on drugs, clutching guidebooks and talking only about how to get the cheapest price for everything. I had already seen instances of this preoccupation with screwing the utmost from the local economy. A foreign man I previously shared a tuk tuk ride with complained bitterly and argued furiously about paying the equivalent of a dollar, as though it was a very serious matter. It was the nasty and aggrieved way that he did it that annoyed me. A few cents more or less is not a matter of life or death to someone who can afford to travel.

The bus station was a huge, open affair consisting of many rows of red plastic chairs covered by a roof. I had decided on the VIP bus. It was air-conditioned and reputed to make less stops and take less time than the ordinary bus. Despite this it was not costly, and because of its VIP title it was not as full. (The hippies as a matter of pride take the lesser bus.) Inside the bus the seats were elevated a little from the undercarriage, and down three deviously twisting steps in the centre of the vehicle was a tiny toilet, difficult to manoeuvre into on a jolting bus but extremely welcome when the need arose. It was the narrowest size imaginable, like a shortened coffin. After wrestling the door open and ducking my head to enter, I found myself encapsulated in something built for a pygmy where crouching stance only was permitted.

The first hour of travelling took us through closely built housing that soon gave way to scattered villages and rice paddies. Later there were forest-covered hills and mountains interspersed with pockets of taro or banana cultivation – small patches that had been scratched out wherever a bit of flat land was available.

The bus stopped a couple of hours into the journey. This was nicotine time for the addicts, and also a chance for the male passengers to head for the bushes. I was pleased to find that Laos had embarked on an anti-smoking crusade. Travelling on buses and trains was now more comfortable than in the bad old days when being gassed went with the price of a ticket on public transport. A Lao woman also got off for a toilet break, but she didn't seek the bushes with the men. She parked herself in full view alongside the bus on the road verge, relying on the decency of people not to look. I saw her lift her sarong to display bulky Bombay bloomers, loose knee-length white cotton pantaloons, before hastily averting my eyes.

After this the road travelled through large areas of forest where there was no sign of houses or cultivation. Much of Laos is mountainous, relatively uninhabited terrain covered by impenetrable jungle cut by rivers and ravines. The mountains, restricting access and progress, are the reason that Laos remains the least densely populated country Asia, with just over 6.7 million people.

It was a lush-looking land. The only places I saw that were not green were the patches of hillside that had been stripped down to the bare bones of the earth by loggers. Sad to see; much illegal logging happens in Laos.

Then the karsts began, those intriguing limestone peaks that rise abruptly out of flat earth and go straight up like a pointing finger. At one place a mini karst crouched right beside the road. Fat and squat, about four metres high, its black background was picturesquely splashed with streaks of white and ochre. In front of it stood a brightly painted yellow and red spirit house complete with offerings of flowers and fruit. A very potent presence indeed would inhabit such a beautiful and auspicious rock.

The town of Vang Vieng, noted for the beauty of its

surroundings, is located in the midst of this scenic karst country, but, being currently uninterested in serious partying, the town's reputation as hippie heaven put me off a visit. Later, when I had reviewed the literature on the subject and learned that there are places to stay apart from the dropout centres, I thought I might try it next time around.

I also put the Plain of Jars, a little to the north-east of here, on the list for next time. At this site hundreds of large jars carved from solid stone, most weighing from a half to one tonne, are scattered mysteriously across an extended area of empty fields. Thought to be around two thousand years old, they lie inscrutably awaiting recognition, mute testimony to an origin and function lost in time.

Along the way I saw few vehicles on the road apart from the odd truck or tuk tuk, and occasionally we passed one of those funny tractor carts I had seen in outlying parts of China. Called 'dok doks' because that is the noise they make, they are used to ferry village goods and people about in country areas.

The bus ride was long and rough. Laos has few roads, many of which are unpaved. This route between Vientiane and Luang Prabang is Laos's main highway. It runs all the way to China, and although now it has a sealed surface it still delivered a callisthenic workout with the effort required of passengers to remain upright. Especially so when we came to the mountains and the road became a narrow twisty track of frequent serpentine bends. Before this road was built the Mekong had been the principal means of travel, not only in the north but also throughout the country. Initially I had hoped to travel by river from Vientiane to Luang Prabang, but on enquiry I found that although it was possible it was not easy to find a boat, and the cost was only practical if several people shared the ride.

However, the Mekong is still the way to travel from Luang Prabang to Thailand. That is on my list for next time. I have no wish to see Sungai Kolok or Nong Khai ever again. One such border crossing experience is quite enough to last a lifetime thank you.

At about the halfway mark, four and half hours on, we drew up at a village for a chance to restore our tissues with food and indulge in a comfort call. The toilet block was spacious and sparkling, with plenty of water in large tiled tubs for the dipper flush and a hose on the wall instead of loo paper. After my visit, I sat down on a stone bench that surrounded a circular stone table, and food was produced. I was given a big bowl of soup in which various items floated – I made sure none were pig's blood masquerading as tofu this time – and another bowl of vegetables and pork. The meat was mostly fat and bone and I sneaked it onto the floor for the resident cat, which had materialised along with the food, intent on making my acquaintance.

Still failing to find peanuts in the lineup of packets on the stalls at the front of the cafe, I bought some dried chips of what I hoped was sweet potato and moved on to another bench to eat them with a young Australian couple who were also travelling on the bus. Now the resident dog came to sit beside me, looking hopeful. I did not oblige, so I got a few taps on the leg to remind me of my obligations. The animals here looked well fed. In fact all the cats and dogs I had seen so far appeared OK. The dogs were small to medium sized and a mixture of beagle/spaniel types, though some could have had a slight ancestry of dingo.

Back on the bus, and the road continued to wind among, and up and down, mountains, but the driver went carefully. I saw none of those gut-wrenching drops over the side that

I had found so nerve-wracking elsewhere in mountainous territory.

Finally, in the late afternoon, nine and a half hours after leaving Vientiane, we arrived at Luang Prabang's southern bus station, a vast concern where a host of tuk tuks awaited custom. Several travellers from the bus and I were shuffled into one and charged 10,000 kip for a ride to a guesthouse. One Englishman whined all the way to the town about the exorbitant price of $1.20.

The tuk tuk toured the town showing the other passengers guesthouses until they were all accommodated. Then I was delivered to the Sayo, the guesthouse that I had pre-booked using my new phone connection. In narrow Xieng Mouane Street, a step from the river in the temple district, the Sayo is a faded former French colonial mansion. My room was huge and stuffed full of ponderous antique wooden furniture, some of which had functions that eluded me. One cupboard contained clothes hangers but was so low I had to kneel on the floor to put my shirt in it. The room had an exceedingly high ceiling where unfortunately they had seen fit to install the light globe when electricity had come to town. And as this room was on the ground floor, the shutters over the windows that gave onto the street outside were closed for privacy, so the room was depressingly dim. I felt no good vibes here.

I flopped down onto the bed for a rest, then later went cruising the street outside for food. There were several cafes close by, all with sidewalk dining. I must have picked an expensive one as my excellent three-course meal cost a whole twelve dollars.

Strolling back to the Sayo in the warm night air I paused to check out some alternative lodgings and found one I really liked. Only two doors from the Sayo, it was a guesthouse called Xieng Mouane, after the street it is in. Another big colonial villa – white painted with grey wooden shutters – the Xieng Mouane Guesthouse had an uninspiring front behind which hid a delightful courtyard garden, a profusion of greenery dotted with little lights. Just off the street in the tiny foyer I found Madame, the proprietor, reclining on a bamboo couch watching TV. She led me across the garden, up a roofed wooden staircase and onto a tiled verandah, and showed me a room whose balcony overlooked the garden. It had lots of light and cost much less than the dim cavern in which I was currently entombed at the Sayo. I booked it for the next day.

7 In quest of Hotel Peppery

I slept in the Sayo's enormous, heavy wooden four-poster bed under a voluminous tent of mosquito netting, and was up and ready to move by nine. The guesthouse manager did not seem amused that I wanted to depart his establishment, but of course he was polite about it. He tried to convince me to take other rooms but there was something I didn't like about the atmosphere of this place. Maybe it was haunted. But that normally wouldn't put me off. I like old houses, haunted or not.

I moved into my new room two doors along the street and was happy. It had no TV but otherwise all mod cons. Birds singing in the garden and orchids hanging over the balcony more than made up for that. The rules posted beside the door of this room were identical to those found in other guesthouses and hotels in Laos. Government orders, demonstrating that august body's low opinion of visitors. They read –

TOURIST TO BE IN OWN ACCOMMODATION 2300
(I believe this curfew is enforced in all places but I was flat out staying awake until ten let alone eleven after a hard day doing my Good Little Tourist stuff.)

FOR MAKING SEX MOVIE IN THE ROOM, IT IS RESTRICTION!
(Oh poo, there go my holiday snaps.)

IT IS NOT ALLOW BRING AMMUNITION INTO ROOM EXCEPT THE OFFICIAL WHO HAVE PERMISSION ONLY.

(This somehow did not give me reassurance. A lot of liquored-up gun-toting soldiers sprang to mind.)

NOT ALLOW ANY DRUGS, CRUMBLING OR BRING MAN OR WOMAN INTO HOTEL WHO IS NOT WIFE OR HUSBAND FOR MAKING LOVE.

(Prostitution is illegal in Laos and so is fraternisation or inappropriate behaviour between Lao and foreigners, but a bit of crumbling I am personally all for.)

IF YOU DO NOT FOLLOW THE ACCOMMODATION REGULATION YOU WILL BE FIGHT BASED ON LAO LAW PDR.

DO NOT TAKE HOTEL PEPPERY WHEN YOU LEAVE.

(If I had been able to actually find some peppery I might have been tempted – it sounds so intriguing.)

ANY RESTAURANT WEDDING SOCIAL PARTIE OF ANY KIND MUST STRICLY ABIDE BY THE RULES – 2300 – ANYONE WHO VIOLATES THIS RULE WILL BE EDUCATED AND FINED 500,00 – SERIOUS WILL BE ENFORCED BY LAW.

NO PERSON UNDER 18 IS NOT PERMITTED TO ENTER SOCIAL PARTIE IF FOUND BY RESPONSIBLE OFFICER WILL BE FINED AND EDUCATED.

FOREIGNER OR LAO IN THE STREET WITHOUT IDENTITY CARD OR LATE PAST 2300 WILL BE FINED AND EDUCATED FOR VIOLATING THE RULE.

SIGNED LP PUBLIC SECURITY UNIT LAO PDR

The literature I read before I came to Laos had made it quite clear that the government frowns on 'inappropriate behaviour between Lao and foreigner'. This seems to mean any form of physical contact – dancing too closely or public displays of affection can be seen as an offence. There wasn't the sleazy sex tourism you see in some countries. Another warning for travellers is that possession of even a small amount of a drug will incur a heavy fine, and it is forbidden to photograph any place that could have military significance, such as airports. From a tourist's view point though I did not feel constricted or oppressed at any time in my Lao stay.

Out to investigate Luang Prabang on my first morning, I found the weather to be unbelievably, gaspingly hot. In the rainy season the maximum temperature gets to around 38°C (100°F) and the humidity is almost as high. The sky was overcast; there was that ominous feeling of waiting for a storm to break, waiting for the relief of rain. Even so I walked for a couple of hours in order to get my bearings.

I was enchanted by Luang Prabang. It is like no other place I have ever been. I felt as though I had stepped out of a time capsule. Everywhere I looked in this slow-moving, non-polluted town there were interesting, hundred-year or more old French colonial buildings, some gracefully declining into shabby chic, and dazzling temples, some over five hundred years old. There are apparently thirty-six temples in the town but I got tired of trying to count them. Surrounding everything were luscious gardens, lofty palms and large flowering shade trees.

Situated at the junction of the Mekong and Nam Khan rivers, encircled by mountains at 700 metres above sea level, Luang Prabang, the former capital of Laos, is still its religious and artistic centre. Listed as a World Heritage preservation site by UNESCO in 1995, it is unique and the jewel in Lao's crown. Despite being a magnet for tourists, it manages to retain its ancient ambience, possibly due to the fact that it is one of the most remote towns in the country.

First I explored the area where I was staying. Xieng Mouane Street runs along a small peninsula of land known as the temple district, which lies between the two rivers. Now and then a few of Luang Prabang's population of 26,000 ambled past me at a sedate pace. Across the narrow street from my guesthouse were two stunning temple complexes standing in peaceful extensive gardens, Wat Choum Khong and Wat Xieng Mouane. At the end of the street were the grounds of the royal palace, now a museum. From there it was a short walk to the main street, the tourist hub, which was lined with cafes, small shops and tour offices.

It was wonderful to think that the plan of these tiny thoroughfares that I now walked on had not changed since the fourteenth century. Built then for foot traffic, now they had only room enough for mopeds – the ubiquitous small motorbikes – to negotiate along them. Local pride was evident. All along the diminutive lanes in front of the petite houses were tiny garden plots and terracotta pots filled with plants.

At night the main street transforms itself into a colourful market that meanders along for a considerable distance under multihued umbrellas. I wandered up and down the brilliant display, pleased to find that the sellers didn't hassle me as they do in some other countries. The offerings were mostly handcrafts, textiles, silver or wood. There were so many pretty and novel items to be inspected, it took me ages to get around it.

All the restaurants and cafes were open but I chose to eat at the market's food stalls located in a narrow side alleyway. I bought a large chunk of boned chicken ingeniously skewered between the prongs of a bamboo stick shaped like a tuning fork. You chew down both sides and then release the rattan tie holding the prongs together to get the last bit. The chicken came served on a piece of banana leaf – no washing up or unbiodegradable litter. I joined a row of other diners on a skinny wooden bench against the low wall of the alley to eat my chicken. After a while I sensed a presence behind me; a tiny tabby kitten draped along the top of the wall, and almost at my shoulder, gazed soulfully at me. Naturally I gave him a share of my dinner. Also on offer at these stalls was a special – 'All you can put in a bowl'. For sixty-five cents you took a bowl and piled whatever you fancied into it from a row of other bowls arranged along a trestle. My dinner was the expensive sort. It cost one dollar twenty five.

After eating, I took one of the short cuts that I am so fond of – which rarely end up being anything of the kind – and instead of returning to the market I continued along the food alley to its other end. Then I was in a dark narrow lane that wound around among tiny unlit backstreets, and here I saw how the Lao live. It seemed to be mostly outside, by the light that spilled from open doorways. Men sat on stools playing draughts using beer bottle tops as counters while mother squatted on her haunches cooking the evening meal over a clay brazier filled with coals. The meal was eaten at wooden tables and benches that were also outside, or on sleeping mats on the tiled floor of the front (and often only) room of the house.

Open to the street, I could see into these rooms. They had little furniture, sometimes just a TV in an almost bare space. No one seemed to worry about theft. The pretty spirit houses on poles outside the dwellings of the lanes wouldn't last five minutes at home. Someone nicked my trowel in the few moments I left it alone and unchaperoned on the verge of my quiet street in suburban Adelaide. Here the streets have lovely pottery urns, lamp holders and pot plants – all for the picking up.

I walked for a considerable time in these meandering back lanes and in the end I came out back exactly where I had started from in the market.

Later that night it rained heavily and thank goodness it was cooler in the morning. By two in the afternoon it was still pouring. Oh, the joy of sitting on my room's verandah, among the trees and plant pots and hanging baskets of orchids, an all-green world, watching tropical rain fall down in a straight, solid line. We had been rain deprived for so long at home I couldn't get enough of it now. How I wished I could take some back to Australia with me.

First thing next morning I took a tuk tuk to the day market. On the couple of streets of the town wide enough to allow traffic, there was very little of it and it was mostly jumbo, tuk tuk, bicycle or moped – all travelling very slowly. Cars were rare and buses or trucks are forbidden; and the road from Vientiane bypasses the town. Most of the cars I did see were vintage; especially impressive were two elderly Mercedes in lovingly cared for condition.

The day market was enormous. Sprawling over an extensive area, it had clothes, produce and household goods. The one-person-wide walkways between the rows of stalls were wet and muddy underfoot after the rain. Many stalls displayed the same range of goods and much of it seemed to be in miniature – tiny bags of washing powder and small bottles of shampoo. Nearby I found a pharmacy where anything your heart desired (almost) could be had for a price. This establishment's till was a plastic bucket that swung on a rope from a ceiling hook. The assistant tugged the bucket towards her, casually threw the takings into it, scrabbled among the notes for change, then shoved it aside.

Another tuk tuk ferried me on to the Palace Museum.

Only in a communist country do you get to prance freely through a complete royal palace. (Although I did once get inside a prison in Bolivia, I guess that's not quite the same.) After the obligatory removal of my footwear outside the door, I entered a room on one side of the building. In this room was a wall of small wooden cupboards, some with keys hanging in the locks of their doors. I selected one, deposited my bag and pocketed the key, taking care not to touch a group of young visiting monks who were milling about in there also leaving their belongings. An attendant seated behind a desk in the palace doorway took my 30,000 kip entry fee and I trod soundlessly inside on the marble floor.

The palace was built in 1904 as the residence of King Sisavang Vong and his family. It stands in a walled compound above the river landing where official visitors would disembark to be received. It is a blend of traditional Lao and French styles. Passing through the entry hall, I found myself in the throne room, which, to put it mildly, was absolutely fabulous. The walls were completely covered with stunning decoration – carved gilded wood for the first metre up from the floor, then a deep-red painted background overlaid with spectacular coloured-glass mirror mosaics soaring all the way to the high ceiling. Not surprisingly, the mosaics took eight craftsmen three and a half years to complete. In the centre of the room sat the king's gilded throne and around it were royal vestments and gold and silver sabres.

Three massive chandeliers hung in the span of the main hall. Worth a fortune, they impressed me no end, but you'd never get up again if one fell on you. However, the two small Austrian crystal basket-shaped ones in the glass pavilions that housed collections of priceless gold and crystal Buddha statues were exactly the same as two I once had. It's a bit of a letdown to discover that a palace is content to use anything ordinary enough for me to own. (But even the

Queen's cornflakes are served out of a Tupperware container I have heard.)

Against the walls of another reception room stood glass cases containing thousands more Buddha statues of all sizes. Another row of display cases stored diplomatic gifts received from other countries. No prizes for spotting the Australian present – a boomerang.

Halls behind the reception area led to the living quarters that were used by the last royals, King Sisavang Vatthana and his family. The rooms have been preserved as they were when the royal family was removed in 1975, which ended six hundred and fifty years of Lao monarchy. Some Lao believe the spirits of the departed family still haunt these rooms.

The palace also houses the Pha Bang or Prabang Buddha, the town's namesake. Made of cast gold, silver and bronze, it is almost a metre high and weighs 53.4 kilogram's. Since its presentation to the Lao king sometime in the 12th century, it has been regarded as a symbol of religious and political authority, bestowing the right to rule the country on the holder. It has been captured and removed several times and no one is sure if this is the genuine article or a replica. Rumour has it that the real one is possibly in Moscow or hidden somewhere in Vientiane. It seems unlikely the communists would have left something like this hanging around when they took over in 1975. Whatever it is, the benign-looking Buddha is still Luang Prabang's most revered and precious icon.

Back in the street, I walked all the way around the base of Mount Phousi, the high pointy mountain that rises steeply beside the palace in the centre of town. It is considered sacred and a climb to its summit constitutes a pilgrimage. The mountain is crowned by a golden stupa that can be seen from all over town, like a pimple on a pumpkin, especially at night when it is lit in a golden blaze of light. I wondered if my circumambulation of the base of the site could count as a visit. I didn't think I would make it up the hundreds of almost perpendicular steps to the top.

Instead I went to My Library where I donated two packs of books. This is a worthy charity providing books for village children. You buy the books from them and they send them to a needy school. Books come next after food in my scale of necessary equipment for survival.

Then I made another attack on the internet and finally mastered it. The attendant in the office gave me some good advice: to use my mobile phone to call home since it is half the price of being connected through the internet (and to forget the hopeless landlines.) To my utter amazement it worked and the family in Australia came through as clear as a bell.

The next day started with another cool morning after much rain in the night, but by eleven when I had been out and walking since eight-thirty, I was hot and sweaty. I ate lunch at the Phousi Guesthouse at the end of my street. A male foreigner came downstairs bare-chested and barefoot, clad only in shorts. I found this revolting. Don't they read the guidebook? They all go about clasping it to their bosoms like a drowning man clutching a life buoy. It's their Holy Bible. But they must either skip the bits about how to behave so as not to offend local custom or else think that it doesn't apply to them.

For lunch I ordered an omelette, passing on the 'fired coyote stuffed with fired swamp glory', but something went awry in the translation to the cook and the omelette appeared as two boiled eggs. They still had their tops on and I was given only a very tiny plastic spoon with which to attack them. I managed. Nothing comes between my food and me.

In the afternoon it rained again and I sat once more on the cool verandah outside my room looking out at the garden, listening to the steady plop plop of water falling from tree leaves onto the tiled roof. What a blissful sound. A tall jackfruit tree grew beside the verandah, with several massive fruit hanging on it by long thick stems. Jackfruit have a rough outer skin like a loofah and, the size and shape of a football (Australian that is), are the biggest fruit I have seen on a tree. The courtyard and quadrangle of garden the rooms faced had a central lawn surrounded by palms, stone jars, pot plants, and in its centre was a three-tiered sandstone fountain into which the rain now splashed. Everything including the verandah was laced with creepers and overhung by frangipani trees and huge frothy bamboo palm fronds. There was no electricity in the garden and the small lights that dot it and make it a fairyland by night were solar. Everything was green, quiet and peaceful. It was a delightful place.

Towards evening and after a solid siesta I ventured out again. Seeing an enticing advert, I stopped for a foot massage. A young girl was the masseuse and the modus operandi was for the massagee to lie semi-relined on a cushioned couch just off the footpath, where all the action was clearly visible to the passers-by. This foot massage was different from the Thai one I'd enjoyed in the Bangkok train station. It lasted an hour and it included a neck pummelling. It hurt only a little and it refreshed my feet enough to enable them to make it all the way around the peninsula by the riverside path.

The narrow riverfront road was very pleasant to stroll along. Little traffic uses it, and if you follow it all the way around you come back to where you began. Now and then, at the edge of the water and high on the top of the bank, there were small cafes to refresh yourself or seats to just sit and contemplate. Several flights of steps led down to boat landings. On the opposite side of the road were houses and small guesthouses, and at the end was a large and magnificent temple, Xieng Thong.

My guesthouse went all the way through from its narrow street to this riverfront one and had a back gate with a bell that you could ring to be let in to save you walking around to the front entrance. All the architecture beside the road was ancient, colonial or quaint. I enjoyed this walk no end. At a fruit stand I stopped for bananas. Fifty cents for a hand, they were short, fat, solid, tree-ripened and utterly delicious.

I couldn't fail to notice that with affluence and tourists had come plastic and disposables. I wondered about rubbish collection here. Big bamboo baskets of it sat hopefully on some street corners and at others rubbish-filled plastic bags were piled high. Did it ever get picked up? Rubbish was also free ranging, strewn along the edge of the river and other public places – a distressing sight. But I did see a woman collecting empty plastic water bottles, of which there must be millions. (Drinking the water from the tap is not for those without a death wish.) This lady had a moped onto which she deftly tied four huge, bulging black plastic bags of bottles, two each side. She then mounted with great care and rode off extremely precariously, wobbling like an overloaded bumblebee.

8 Watch out your hairs

It rained a steady drip, drip all afternoon, and, revelling in the cool respite from the heat, I hoisted my umbrella and went walking. I had dinner at a nearby guesthouse and went to bed early. The rain increased, pouring down heavily during the night, but had almost stopped by eight in the morning when I had to venture out. I had booked a ride on a local riverboat to visit Pak Ou, the Caves of the Buddha, three hours and twenty-five kilometres upriver.

In gently spitting rain I walked to the tour boat's office, only a little distance away in the same street as my guest-house. I was then shoved onto the back of a moto and bounced around the corner to a riverside boat landing to join a few other cave seekers already assembled there. We settled in for the obligatory wait, then, gingerly making our way down a high flight of muddy, slippery steps, we clambered into the boat, a long, narrow wooden object with two wooden bench seats separated by a skinny aisle. The driver sat apart up in the pointed prow. The boat was painted light sky-blue like almost all the 'slow' passenger boats on the river. The fast boats you don't want to know about. They are speedboats – loud, noisy and extremely dangerous.

The boat's roof was so low I had to hunker down to manoeuvre along the cramped walkway between the seats. A sign on one crossbar warned, 'Watch out your hairs'.

Unfortunately this was usually seen far too late and many hairs were cracked as we scrambled to our seats.

Then we were off. The rain had stopped, the sun was out and it was lovely to be on the water, shaded and comfortable, in the cool breeze. The river was muddy brown and fast-flowing, but not so wide that both banks could not be seen clearly. As soon as the town was left behind, there were no houses or villages visible, only dense green foliage and impenetrable-looking forest. The land on either side of the river rose steeply up from precipitous banks behind which stood lofty mountains, their tops obscured by cloud and mist. Behind these mountains are vast pockets of unexplored territory and remote hill tribes, descendants of settlers from Tibet and south-west China who moved into the rugged hill country because it suited their traditional methods of farming opium, corn and domestic animals.

The boat's driver kept close to the edge of the riverbank. We were pushing upstream against the flow and there was less pull there. On the return journey he took a course down the middle of the river. At times we skirted around dangerous-looking whirlpools and viciously tugging currents.

Many boats travelled the river, chugging up and down stream. In this northern part of Laos the river is still the main highway. Barges do most of the work, and although only a few long-distance passenger boats operate regularly boat travel is still the means of transport to and from villages along the river. The bigger craft were like those I had seen in the Mekong Delta of Vietnam, rather like small Chinese junks. There were also tiny pirogues, canoes that are paddled along. They are extremely flat and have practically no draught so that from a distance the rower appears to be sitting directly on the water. I saw one in which two people sat with a dog between them, perched in a row like beer bottles on a wall.

I saw no roads or riverside landing places that could be signs of villages until we drew up to a small wooden jetty from which steps cut into a steep bank ascended to a village perched high above the water. This was Ban Xang Hai, its name means the 'jar maker's village', but it is now known as the whisky village and the stop here meant that we were expected to buy some of this local rice-fermented fire-water called *lao-lao*.

Home to seventy people, Ban Xang Hai's inhabitants originally did make jars, but now they get the jars from elsewhere and fill them with the spirits they make. This village is an ancient settlement. Recent archaeological excavations here have produced jars that date to around two thousand years ago. And a cave on the opposite side of the river yielded artifacts that are around eight thousand years old. It has also deposits of gold. In the dry season, when the sandbars in the middle of the Mekong are exposed, the villagers paddle out there and pan for gold.

The village headman exhibited his immaculately neat village to us with obvious pride. He escorted us to its centerpiece, a small square containing a pretty temple and a stupa with the usual predominance of gold. Displayed on bamboo and wooden benches nearby was not only the celebrated whisky but also local handcrafts. This was our cue to spend up big. Also taking advantage of the needs of tourists, a red arrow pointed to a stone hut. Inside I found a squeaky-clean hole-in-the-floor loo and a big tank of brown river water alongside it complete with a plastic dipper. This was the village's communal bathhouse. I used it gratefully and the privilege cost me two thousand kip (twenty-five cents) collected by an aged custodian who materialised as I came out. An exorbitant price by local standards but well worth it I considered.

My most pressing needs having been catered for, I did

my duty and spent some money. Whisky does not interest me, so I bought two rather wonderful ethnic necklaces for a few dollars. Then a tiny girl convinced me to buy a set of three miniature dolls dressed in Lao traditional costumes made from local fabrics. I try not to buy souvenirs and I certainly didn't want this lot but I couldn't resist the sweet child's gentle entreaty. Considering all the work that had gone into the making of the dolls, they cost a pittance at a few cents each.

I was allowed back to the boat now that I had done my duty and been a Good Little Tourist and we continued on. Now there was evidence of logging on the mountainsides, scars and patches appeared that at first I thought were a sort of lawn-like grass until I realised that they were low regrowth. I could still not see any roads so I wondered how they got the logs out. Maybe they slid them into the river and floated them down, as I believe the French did in the past further south.

At about the halfway mark we passed a big prison. It looked completely isolated and a difficult place from which to escape, as though its only access would be from the river.

Then, at the point where the Mekong meets the Nam Ou River, we came to Pak Ou, the sacred Caves of the Buddha. These are two large bites taken out of a high rocky limestone cliff that rises straight up vertically from the riverside. The main cave is not very deep but it is wide, and from its gaping mouth thousands of Buddha images, large and small, dating from the 16th century, gaze out serenely on the passing waters of the river.

Labouring up a long precipitous set of stone steps, I reached the cave entrance where I forked over the required fee to one of the female guardians in attendance. Because I dropped an extra donation into an alms bowl that stood on their table, one of the ladies gave me a small bundle of incense sticks tied with a sliver of banana leaf and decorated with an orange marigold. The woman then gestured toward the shrine that stood beside the entrance. In it resided several gilded Buddhas before whom offerings were being made. I took off my shoes and, with my hands pressed together in the traditional *nop*, made the required three bows, lit my incense sticks and stuck them in the sand of the silver bowl in front of the images.

Moving further into the cave I found that it was literally crammed, filled to bursting, with Buddhas. There were hordes of people in there, already far too many people for my liking, but they were predominately Lao and Thai pilgrims who behaved with decorum. Then an expensive tourist boat arrived and bedlam broke out. A tourist feeding frenzy took place! Their boat was exceedingly fancy – its carved wooden seats had backrests and cushions. It even had a loo and a hostess. But the people on it were awful. I was heartily glad I hadn't come with them. Of a European variety that shall not be named, they were elderly and should have known better than to carry on the way they did. Horrible noisy brutes, they shouted and laughed and blocked the steps like a bunch of dimwitted chooks, flapping and squawking about with no regard for the fact that this cave is a very holy place to the local people. People shushed them but they remained blissfully unaware.

I took a quick look around the cave and shot back to my boat to wait its return. The river ride had been great but the badly behaved tourists ruined the cave visit. As the present time was the rainy and therefore the off-tourist season, I decided that it must be pandemonium here in the on season.

Back at Luang Prabang I fell ashore faint from near starvation and headed for the first cafe on the riverbank. I ordered fish steak, feeling sure that this fish deal wouldn't include fins, head or tail. It didn't, but it did come with all its bones. And very big ones too, indicating that the steak had been previously part of one of the large Mekong catfish that are caught locally. I had read that they are the biggest fresh-water fish in the world. The first I knew about the bones was when I found that for some reason I couldn't seem to get my mouth shut – I had a large piece of bone skewered through my tongue. Then the pain struck! I pulled the offending bone out fast and proceeded on, carefully negoti-ating around the hazards.

The fish was scrumptious. I also ordered my favorite local specialty, green papaya salad. I eat this dish whenever I visit Darwin's night market where they ask, 'One, two or three?' when you order it. This means how many chillies do you want? According to your taste the spices and chillies are then ground in a mortar and pestle and mixed with the salad. Laos's papaya salad just came with a hot three.

That evening, after a saunter down the tourist drag and through the night market, I decided to return to my guest-house a different way. I must have turned in the wrong direction at the riverbank and instead of coming out near the back end of my street I came out in a part of the town I hadn't been before – the far end of the tourist strip. I had gone around in a circle to get there.

Seeing a travel agent's office, I popped in to see if I could change my plane ticket to go home from Bangkok instead of Singapore. The man in charge had never heard of Qantas (sorry Qantas!), but on the wall, on the list of the airlines they did deal with was, in large red letters, Ansett Australia. I tried to tell him that poor Ansett was long dead, but he didn't believe me. I wonder if he is still booking passengers on them.

This manager person was an authoritative older man. He

ordered me, 'You must go this way', and 'you must do that'. I said, 'Bossy, isn't he?' to the young assistant sitting nearby, who giggled furtively. Bossy ordered me to return the next day. And I did. This man didn't brook argument.

In a mini-mart near the travel office I bought vanilla yoghurt (I found no plain natural yoghurt in Lao) and cheese. Pineapples were for sale everywhere on street stalls. It was their harvesting time at present. It was also school holiday time, which is always arranged to coincide with harvesting or rice-planting times so the kids can help with the work. Poor little beggars.

9 Soft adventure with elephant

Next morning I was up early and ready for elephants! I had booked an excursion to a camp that was a sort of Pachyderm Retirement Home for the elderly, unemployed or homeless of the species. The day before I had visited The Elephant House on the riverfront just around the corner from my street. This elephantalia centre had exhibits, a multimedia library, a coffee bar and a boutique that sold elephant poo paper (not for wiping elephant bottoms but made out of their droppings) and other elephant-related trappings.

I read the brochure listing the delights of a day out consorting with elephants. It offered:

Seated on elephant howdah for starting off soft adventure.

Seated off from howdah.

Take pleasure with lunch on beautiful scenic.

Arrive back Luang Prabang with safe and sound.

What more could I ask? I had signed on the dotted line immediately for this enticingly described 'soft adventure' that promised to convey me back from it intact and 'with safe and sound'!

At the office I visited their toilet. Laos's toilets are not the elusive article that they prove to be in many other countries. And not only that, they are squeaky clean. Happiness is a clean toilet! And no one is surprised or embarrassed when you ask to use theirs. Once I asked to use a small internet office's toilet and was taken into their living quarters at the back of the shop. Sparsely furnished, but shiningly spotless, the room contained nothing except a TV and a big sleeping mat on the floor in front of it. Behind this room was a small kitchen where grandma sat cross-legged on the tiled floor cutting green salad vegetables into a bowl, and off this was a room with the toilet and water tank with dipper for washing.

The excursion I was about to undertake was to the Elephant XL Camp near Xieng Lom village fifteen kilometres from Luang Prabang on the Nam Khan River. Although the Asian elephant is endangered, Laos has the biggest remaining population – around eight hundred live wild in the forests and twelve hundred still have gainful employment. But habitat loss and hunting continues to decrease the numbers of those living wild, while mechanisation loses the workers their livelihood. A mere two thousand are left from the days when Laos was known as the Land of a Million Elephants. Then they were not only labourers but also the battle tanks of warfare and the Rolls Royce of travel vehicles.

The XL Camp was established in 2003 to give redundant, old or sick elephants a safe home and care by vets and experienced mahouts. This project provides jobs for local people; all the staff, guides, cooks and mahouts belong to surrounding villages. It also supports their communities, financing the construction of a water supply, funding the Xieng Lom Village School and carrying on various elephant by-product industries like fertiliser and poo paper.

Eventually two more folk arrived for the elephant trip, a nice young Australian couple, and we took off. Our transport to the camp was, fittingly, a jumbo, a lumbering mechanical beast with an enclosed front seat and an open back. I climbed into the front seat with the driver, which I soon found to be a mistake. The jumbo had an ancient, hard-used motor and the heat and fumes it gave off rose up from under the dashboard to assault me. And when we came to the mountains my position became the suicide seat. On the return journey I made sure I rode in the open rear, which was much cooler and less stressful.

We set off on the main – and only – road to the south, the Vientiane Road, and after grinding along a short way stopped for petrol. It cost $1.50 a litre. Not far from the town I saw a woman kneeling at the side of the road beside a child who lay curled on a cloth. The way she hung over him and the concern on her face told me that he was sick. He was about eight years old; too big for her to carry. Perhaps she had been taking him to medical aid and had had to stop there to rest. How sad I couldn't help.

Half an hour later we turned off onto a dirt road that, due to the recent rain, was now mostly mud and puddles. Then we started to climb and the road became merely a narrow track beside some pretty stupendous drops over the side. Fortunately, due to the senility of our straining motor, we chugged along very slowly. Everything was beautifully green and there were few houses. Now and then, where patches of flat land occurred at the base of mountains, rice paddies and plots for pineapples had been made. The paddies were filled with water in which men, women and children waded knee-deep, bent over planting rice shoots. At one place a man guided a hand plough that was pushed by a tractor *duc duc* – like a dok dok but without the passenger seats. All the children laughed and waved to us.

There was also evidence of logging on the mountainsides. Where clearing had been carried out there was regrowth but it was only low greenery. I could discern no new trees.

We came to the place from where we had to cross the river to reach the elephant camp. We collected a guide, climbed down a long flight of steps to the water and a delightful fifteen-minute ride in a motorised canoe later arrived at a landing on the other side. Then the fun started. The long steep path up the riverbank was pure mud. There were no handholds or steps to assist the unstable on their feet. You guessed it, that means me. I slipped and slid all over the place and in the end had to be hauled bodily along by our guide.

Finally reaching the top, I was in a clearing surrounded by forest on the edge of the riverbank. On one side stood the mahouts' wooden house and in the centre was a mounting stand – a roofed bamboo platform up a set of steps. Several elephants were tethered around the site. I climbed to the top of the platform and a mahout rode an elephant over to stand beside it so that I could swing into the howdah on its back.

My elephant and I and the mahout, a young man who sat on her neck, set off on a trail that led through the teak forest. The track we followed was almost entirely mud and the elephant slowly and carefully trod her way along it, her feet making loud suction noises each time she picked one up. The mahout talked softly to her now and then, encouraging her along. I held my brolly aloft, first for the sun and, later, when we went deeper into the forest where it was dark and gloomy, for the light rain that started to fall. There wasn't much to see apart from the odd butterfly – small butter-yellow ones, big black and gold ones, and another that was a light shade of ochre, but it was a terrific experience.

My ride over, I bought an entire hand of bananas, sixty

cents worth, and fed them to my mount. She ate the bananas, skin and all. Dropping one, I marvelled at how daintily she picked it up with her clever trunk. It's hard to believe such a huge animal can be so gentle. The elephants used for rides are all female ex-workers. Females are preferred as workers because they have a more tractable disposition. But I was told to look out for one as I walked past her; she was known to be cranky.

Then I had to negotiate a way back down that awful path to the river. Coming up had been bad enough, but since then there had been more rain and now the path was just a slick mudslide on which it was impossible for me to stand upright, let alone walk. Even clutching the guide's hand I fell flat on my backside – often. By the halfway mark, when the boat driver came to the aid of the guide, I had long given up caring about falling down or my rapidly diminishing self-respect. I gave the driver my other hand and between the two of them they hauled me forcibly down through the mud and into the boat.

On the other side of the river a cleanup was in order. I was a veritable mudpack. The guide seized a hose conveniently attached to a nearby tap, took my shoes and squirted them, then turned the water on me and hosed me down, clothes and all.

Restored to some semblance of decency, if somewhat sodden, I was taken to a nearby eating-place to have the lunch that was included in this jaunt. It wasn't much chop, but it was served, as advertised, 'on beautiful scenic'. This turned out to be high on the edge of the riverbank overlooking the lovely river. Two resident cats came and begged for their share of my food. They were in good condition but still not fussy eaters. They scoffed down all the unappetizing salad I didn't want, lettuce, beans, carrot – everything.

Back in the boat again we travelled further upriver to

see Tat Kuang Si, a wide, many-tiered waterfall. The ride on the river was, after the elephant, the most pleasant experience of the day but the falls were great too. Among incredibly picturesque surroundings an abundance of clear water cascades went, frothing and spraying, over a succession of limestone formations to surge down into a series of limpid pools that were edged and shaded by luxuriant green vegetation. As I stood marvelling at the colossal outpouring of water rushing away from here to continue on to the sea, I couldn't help thinking that just one day's supply might save the River Murray back home! I wished I could take some; they would have never missed it.

10 Sin days

In the evening I set out to do as ordered and return to the bossy travel agent. He told me, 'There is no flight from Bangkok.'

'You no listen,' I said, 'I already told you it is Jetstar.'

'Yes,' piped up his female assistant, 'It goes daily at nine-thirty am.'

Always ask a woman! She had zipped it up on the computer in a flash while Bossy Drawers was telling me no such airline existed. Despite this he was still unable to make contact with them. 'You come back,' he ordered.

Another walkabout in a circle brought me to the night market again. I bought a loose, locally-made shirt made of lightly woven cotton, cooler than a T-shirt. It was like one I had found years ago in India that I had loved and worn until it fell apart.

I watched the mobile manicurist at work. She wandered around the market, basket with the paraphernalia of her trade under one arm, tiny stool under the other. When hailed by one of the stallholders she dropped down onto the stool and set to work on the proffered fingernails.

In a nice little restaurant in the main tourist drag I had a great yoghurt drink that they call 'fruit shake' here. The flavours listed were, 'choc, vanilla, stewbry, love' – Love? I wonder.

A Lao dish that was like chop suey gingered up with

chilli followed. As I waited, suddenly all the lights went out! The entire street was obliterated and I sat in total darkness. This surprised no one – it is a common occurrence. A plate of food was placed on my table in the pitch black. I had to feel my way to it and proceed with caution. It was a long time before a candle was produced.

On the way back to my room I took a successful short cut. To my surprise the little lane halfway along the main tourist strip that I had decided to explore led into the grounds of the Xieng Mouane temple opposite my guesthouse. Luang Prabang was a magical place to walk about in the warm night. All the temple grounds were softly lit, and, looking up, from all over town, you could see the floodlit stupa on the top of Phousi, the sacred mountain, shining bright. Strolling past Xieng Mouane temple, glowing golden against the dark velvety sky, I followed the path through the temple garden where small lanterns in pierced pottery shades gleamed bewitchingly among the plants. Stepping out into the street, I was facing the Xieng Guesthouse.

In the morning when I surfaced it was pouring rain, the heaviest yet. It kept up until ten o'clock and the electricity saw this as an excuse for one of its regular time-outs. By lunchtime, when I had walked about in the sunshine that followed the rain for a couple of hours, it became hotter and hotter and I was wishing for rain again.

My neighbours at the guesthouse, a young Irish couple who had arrived the night before, came out onto our shared verandah to talk to me. The girl had had her purse pinched in an internet office. Silly girl, she'd kept all her credit and other cards in it. Never put all your eggs in one basket is a wise maxim. She said it hadn't been a local who stole it, but a fellow tourist. Swine, they will get theirs. Karma will see to that.

I had no luck with the bossy travel agent. He insisted still that there was no such animal as Jetstar. My accomplice, his female assistant, had disappeared and I had no backup, so I quit. Instead, for a fee he let me use his internet service and I made the booking – with the non-existent Jetstar – and paid for the ticket, but not without an hour of frustration and the loss of a handful of bank notes that Bossy removed from me for the privilege.

By then I was faint from hunger and the goodies on the nearby street corner baguette stands beckoned invitingly. The seller started off well, using tongs to pick up the ingredients, but she soon forgot about the niceties and continued the rest of the performance with her bare hands. This was a little disquieting, as on the street there was no sign of a washing facility. My baguette was enormous and contained egg, salad, a local condiment made of a mixture of dried buffalo skin and chilli and lots more. It was so big it needed two hands to manoeuvre it, so I sat down by the side of the road under a tree to munch. Halfway through I struck what I thought was a tough bit of gristle until I discovered I was chewing on the rubber band that had secured the baguette around its corpulent middle.

Just as my feet were about done for, and after looping right past them the first time, I found the gold shops. What a fizz out; everything was as yellow as brass. This colour does mean that the gold is much more valuable but it does not suit western tastes. Nearby I came across the only bar I saw sporting an English name – Martin's Pub – my nephew's name. He would be proud. The sign at the door said that tonight's video would be Star Wars – the first one.

At four in the afternoon I was jolted from my siesta by a deep and resonant booming. It came from the drum that hung in its own little pavilion in the temple grounds across the street. Its pounding was immediately joined by thuds from the drum in the temple next to it. Then the walls of my room began to shake and rattle as all the surrounding temple drums, as well as their gongs, joined in. The barrage continued for ten long minutes.

Sen Of the Perpetual Mop – and the permanent smile – my guesthouse's gorgeous outdoor attendant, wandered along the veranda waging his never-ending war against uncleanliness. He walked with a rolling limp, dragging one foot, suggesting a congenital hip deformity. I asked him what the racket was all about.

'This day Sin Day,' he told me. It wasn't Sunday so I looked up Sin Day in my guidebook. Nothing to do with naughty goings on, Sin days are the 7th, 8th, 14th and 15th of the waning and waxing moon. On these days temple drums are sounded at four in the morning and four in the afternoon. I couldn't wait for the next onslaught in the pre-dawn; the drum across the street was a real thunderer.

Soon after, feeling it was time I did the obligatory camera-wielding tourist temple trek, I set off to perform this rite. I didn't have far to go to start. The large complex of Wat Xieng Mouane, whose lovely garden I was already familiar with, was right at my door. The monks' quarters in this temple contained classrooms for training young monks in the artistic skills needed to restore and maintain Luang Prabang's temples. Wat Choumkhong, next to it, was also just across the street. It was small but very pretty and also had beautiful gardens.

I walked to the end of my street where Wat Xieng Thong, Luang Prabang's most important temple, spreads across the high piece of land on the end of the narrow peninsula. Climbing the grand sweep of steps leading up to the temple grounds from the road, I had a bird's eye view of the river. On the other side of the complex a wide set of steps, flanked by two large white grinning Cheshire cat statues, led down to a boat landing on the water.

Set among peaceful gardens in the extensive grounds were many beautiful buildings with intricate facades, colourful glass murals that sparkled in the sun and curved roofs that swept down gracefully close to the ground. The main temple building was constructed in 1559 and is regarded as the region's best-preserved example of Buddhist art and architecture. Inside it was magnificent. Delicately decorated wooden columns rose to a ceiling covered with wheels of dharma – the Buddha's teaching – stencilled in gold.

Other smaller chapels had walls covered with brilliant mosaics and housed various images of Buddha. One contained the royal funerary urns and the funerary barge, a thirteen-metre long wooden boat with twin *naga* on the prow, their huge gilded snake heads curving down from a height of twelve metres. *Naga* are the serpent protectors of Buddhism.

I was impressed by the Lao attitude to the practice of Buddhism. It is a joyful, normal part of their everyday lives, as natural to them as breathing and not a serious Sunday-only affair.

Starting back up the other side of the peninsula I paused at three more temples, some faded but all romantically sited among overhanging trees and flowers.

Then I was templed out. Time for another massage!

A tuk tuk ferried me across town to the facilities of the Red Cross where I had read a great massage was to be had. I'll never believe those people who write for the guidebook again. I know I keep saying this but I get caught every time. This massage service may be suitable for great hulking football-playing type males but it is definitely not for the gentler sensitivity of females, especially those with even a modicum of modesty.

I found myself naked on the second storey of a large sprawling wooden building in a tiny bare cubicle, separated only from the rough floorboards by a paper-thin mattress of dubious pristineness. The cubicle was divided from the adjoining ones by woven bamboo strip screens and tatty fabric curtains. And the masseur was a young man! There was no shower and little privacy. I'd had to strip in front of a large open window devoid of screen, curtain or glass from where I'd had a good view of the outside world, which no doubt had a good view of me. I had the feeling I was being observed inside the building, too, and the speed with which the masseur appeared as soon as I was wrapped in my towel was suspicious.

Wondering just where I was going to be pummelled next was nerve-wracking; and could he be sneaking peeps under the loose flopping towel that was the only preservation of my maidenly modesty? Though common sense asked why a fine strapping young man like this would be interested in looking at my ancient and deteriorating equipment. Still I was not letting go of that towel. An hour of rather good massage followed, but it was not as fine as the one I had had from the woman in Vientiane who I could allow to get more personal.

I left reeking of tiger balm oil. Vestiges of it clung resolutely to my skin and tendrils of lank, sticky hair trickled down my neck. It was now dusk and as I was no longer assaulted by the sting of the burning daytime sun I walked all the way back to my room. Passing through the guesthouse garden I smelled the wonderful scent of frying garlic, and saw a girl belonging to the family that ran the guesthouse cooking the evening meal outside under the pergola. Stone seats were grouped around a table and on a bench beside it a coal-fuelled brazier burned under a bubbling wok. I thought how sensible it is that much cooking in Laos is done al fresco.

The next day was my last day in Luang Prabang and I could put it off no longer; I had to climb the sacred mountain, Phousi, the marvellous pointing finger in the centre of the town. The entire mountain is dedicated to the Lord Buddha and much merit is gained by making the ascent. Being in undoubtedly short supply of merit, I could not, without considerable guilt, at least attempt it.

On my first day in Luang Prabang I had looked up one hundred metres vertically, craning my neck to see the top, and thought, No way Hose! But now I hitched up my skirts (metaphorically speaking – I haven't worn skirts for years) for the assault.

Setting off early before the great heat of the day built up, I trod the brick-paved steps that were old, cracked and worn and rose ever so steeply – all 328 of them. At the base of the steps women sold offerings, flowers, incense and tiny dark-brown, frantically fluttering birds in little bamboo cages you can release at the top to gain merit. More merit would be gained, I thought, by refraining from putting them in cages in the first place. I didn't buy a bird much as I would have liked to liberate the lot. I was going to be flat out making it to the top without taking a passenger along.

The steps did not go straight up but zigzagged, weaving a green and shaded path among overhanging trees; the entire mountain was covered with native forest. The steps were edged by a white-painted stone wall and every now and then a low pillar was set in it on which the unfit like me could rest.

Halfway up I stopped to admire an old Bodhi tree enshrined on a small flat space with flowering sweet-scented plumeria trees – frangipani, the national flower of Laos – standing guard over it. The Bodhi tree is sacred to Buddhists because it was the tree under which the Lord Buddha gained enlightenment, so this Bodhi grows in a specially-made elevated ornamental stone surround. (Nothing that could possibly be decorated is left to its own devices here.)

It took me several rest stops before, gasping, I staggered finally onto the small flat bit of land that is the summit. Beside me the That Chomsi stupa, golden and gleaming, rose twenty-four metres in the air. You can't touch this holy of holies, but you can place flowers and incense in the nearby grotto where an imprint of the Buddha's foot rests in the stone. I stepped out of my shoes to enter the small temple next to the footprint. It was a simple construction but replete with the usual quota of gold. Beside the stupa was a pavilion containing the temple drum and beside it two red-painted lingams supported a large brass gong.

The drum is struck vigorously every three hours, a time that came about just as I creaked over the last step onto the top. The sound had a startling effect on me. I jumped a metre in the air and almost made a rapid and precipitous descent to the bottom.

Inside the temple I read the advice:

Virtue conquer evil

Do well obtain well

Do bad obtain bad has deep value for human kind and social ideology

Obtain merit by giving alms

The panoramic views from the top of the mountain were great. I looked down on the whole of Luang Prabang, the surrounding mountains, and the Mekong and Nam Khan rivers meandering away into the distance through a green patchwork of fields. A few steps down from the top on a small crest sat a rusting relic – a Russian anti-aircraft gun support, goodness knows how it got up here. A young boy monk had dropped his outer saffron robe and was using it as a merry-go-round, happily swinging back and forth. He might have been a monk but he was still a small boy. I said, 'Sabai di', and he grinned and said something that clearly meant, 'Do you want to have a go?' I declined. Swinging was the last thing I had in mind after all those steps. And I still had to get down.

I started descending the steps on the other side of the mountain and followed them until they turned into a path. On and on the path wound, snaking along the mountainside among the forest. Eventually I came out on the slopes of the mountain's base and passed a cave shrine in which crouched a fat seated Buddha, looking out at the world like a waiting spider. Further on three large white-painted Buddhas appeared in the shrubbery. Then there were more shrines, *nagas* undulating among the bushes, another Buddha's footprint, smaller Buddhas, as well as the intriguing ruins of two of the oldest temples in Luang Prabang, until finally I landed at the beginning of the township.

The first houses I came to were only shacks with sides of falling-down bits of rattan, iron roofs and a hen or two scratching in the dirt beside them. Then the path turned into a lane sheltering a few better houses. A ferocious dog, deeply suspicious of my intentions, rushed up behind me barking furiously. Resisting the urge to flee for my life, I assumed an innocent stroll, and he escorted me loudly from the district, baying at my heels.

And that was it. It had become incredibly hot and sticky on the climb and I was not walking any further. I hailed a tuk tuk and rode back to the Xieng.

I don't know if I achieved any merit this day but I certainly felt I had earned a rest.

11 Soviet style splendor

In the warm late afternoon, after a baking hot day, and mountain climb, that had left me sweating and gasping, I sat on my delightful balcony and watched a storm blow relief in from China. At first, dark-grey cloud obscured one side of the garden while the other was still in sunlight. Then slowly, inch-by-inch, the grey crept over the grass and trees and the garden became darker and darker until all the sunlight had been chased away. Thunder rumbled. A staccato of raindrops hit the neighbour's tin roof, then came pattering along towards me until it was pinging and plunking on the big leaves of the jackfruit tree. Then, with an almighty crash of thunder directly overhead, there was a rush of cool air and the rain was upon us, pelting down in a torrent, washing everything in its path. Wonderful.

The rain cleared by seven that evening and I went out to get fed. Dodging the boys playing shuttlecock in the street outside my guesthouse, I passed the bus office where I discovered that the next day's nine am bus, on which I had bought a ticket back to Vientiane, had been cancelled and I now had to leave at seven instead. O poo. I did not want to leave this lovely restful place at all, and certainly not at that ungodly hour.

The bus company advertised the delights of their journeys on a blackboard in the street. It bragged that they provided a meal, as well as a toilet. Unfortunately what they didn't have was punctuation, so the sign said: Meals Inside Toilet.

This was almost as unappealing as the competition bus company's main street sign that declared: Snake on bus.

What a choice.

Dinner that night was a fantastic Spanish omelette at The Bakery, a cafe in the main street. And because this was considered a breakfast dish, even though it was now the dark of night, I was given breakfast! Cereal, toast, fruit, juice – I ate the lot. Anyone who has got the hang of making a proper breakfast should not be discouraged.

In the street an old woman beggar approached me timidly. I cannot resist giving alms to old women. After all, I am rapidly approaching being one myself. I met only three beggars in Laos, which was nice after some countries where there are many more. Perhaps Laos is not such a bad country to be poor in, or is it that Buddhists are more likely to support those in need?

Returning home, I misjudged the shortcut through the temple grounds and ended up in someone's backyard where the housedog menaced me. Grandma called it off and seemed not at all put out to find a dopey great foreigner bumbling around on her property after dark.

I slept poorly. Whenever I have to get up early I always fear the alarm won't go off. Luddites don't trust machines. Consequently I was, as usual, awake far too early. Downstairs I found a tuk tuk waiting to take me to the bus station. I hadn't told the bus office where I was staying but they obviously knew. I said goodbye to Sen Of the Perpetual Mop with his lovely happy face, and regretfully departed.

At the bus station I found the bus crammed full. The company had cancelled two buses and consolidated us all, tourists and locals, into this one, the alleged VIP service.

There were even people squatting on tiny blue plastic stools in the aisle, one almost sitting in my lap. I watched his head nodding in front of me as he fell asleep. Further and further it fell until with a jolt he collapsed backwards onto my knees.

A quiet but pleasant young English girl was seated beside me. She told me she had been teaching in China for eight months.

The bus was pretty cramped but I survived. We stopped twice. Once was a toilet break. Set back a bit from the road a row of three open-plan dunnies stood on a patch of mud. Obviously they were built by the Dodgy Brothers Construction Company from bits and pieces of any old material that had come to hand, with doors of tin scraps haphazardly covering the openings. A young boy stood before these highly desirable objects collecting two thousand kip from each of the long line of eager patrons who had flocked off the bus. Inside the toilet wasn't the Ritz, but it was well worth twenty-four cents not to have to manoeuvre in and out of the one on the bus (whether or not there was a meal waiting in there.) Attempting to seal the door, I shot the bolt out of its rickety latch. It fell onto the mud of the floor, and it stayed there. I wasn't picking it up. I'd take my chances on the door flying open. I was full of admiration for the enterprising owners of these facilities. They were, by local standards, making a fortune and from a few heaps of old junk.

Coming through the mountains the bus ride was extremely rough because this time the driver was a lead foot. As the bus swept around the curves it swayed a lot. What I could see of the drops over the side of the road, that fortunately from my aisle seat wasn't much, looked horrible. The lunch stop was at a different place from where we had eaten on the way up. I wasn't hungry, as I'd already eaten the baguette I had brought along for company, but

I couldn't waste the lunch voucher that was included with the VIP bus ticket. I gave it to the Irish girl, the one who'd had her purse stolen, who had a regular, non-lunch voucher ticket. Hopefully this would make up some karma for her – and me.

After six hours, at two in the afternoon, we came to Vang Vieng, Hippie Heaven, where a lot of passengers got off. Some of these were girls wearing skimpy singlet tops and very short shorts. I hoped the cold air-conditioning on the bus had frozen them rigid.

I zipped across the aisle to a spare seat. Relief at last, I could stretch out my legs. From then on, having safely made it through the mountains, apart from the occasional karst, the land was fairly flat and we travelled along valleys containing many rice plots. Everywhere planting was under way. Some places looked as though the whole village was out working, lots of children and as many as ten people were bent over moving along the water-filled paddy in a row. Neat bundles of green rice shoots about twenty centimetres long and big enough to hold in one hand stood waiting to be planted beside the plots in neatly-stacked sheaves.

At five we arrived at the bus station in Vientiane where I was accosted by a tuk tuk driver and installed in his vehicle. An old man approached him and after some discussion the driver asked me if I would allow this old man to ride with me. A villager with many bundles and bags and a stack of bamboo poles, he clambered aboard, banging down a big bag of lychees on my feet and depositing the bamboo poles across my knees. I do not think he paid for this trip.

We proceeded to the Lane Xang Hotel, the former pride of the Soviet era. I wanted to see how party officials lived. The building was set back from the street that ran beside the river and was accessed by a broad, sweeping drive that takes you to the impressive front entrance. But the tuk tuk driver wouldn't go to the door. He dropped me at the road instead. I guessed that he was intimidated by the taxis that lurked in wait at one side of the hotel drive. This was the only place in Laos that I saw taxis.

At the Lane Xang, apart from the grand gesture of the doormen sweeping open the front portals for me, the welcome was non-existent. Acres of highly polished terrazzo floor greeted me once I was inside, separating me from the rather severe young man at the reception desk. Was it because I knew that this hotel was built for the communist elite that I felt a chill in the air; and disapproval of me as a decadent westerner? (I never saw another of my breed in here.) No one helped me with my bag or showed me to my room on the third floor. Another guest had to point the way to the lift hidden around a corner.

The Lane Xang was enormous. Everything in it was big, in the Russian manner of the 1960s, and built a bit rough, or rather naïvely, as though local people with no idea about western fittings had been employed to construct it. There was a predominance of heavy wood, lots and lots of it. It's a good thing I like wood. It was possibly teak, light coloured and carved and decorated within an inch of its life. In the lobby a staggering amount of doors, mirrors, cupboards and panels stood heavily and cumbersomely about. Upstairs, the floors, huge, wide expanses of them, were all carpeted wall to wall – not a good idea in the tropics. The carpet was a dingy, depressing and noticeably unclean pale grey. A damp, manky smell permeated the mile-wide corridor that led to my room.

My large, thirty-dollar room's main focus was also on size. It had a full-length wall of windows through which I could see the Mekong riverside across the road. I stepped through the sliding door in the wall of windows onto a wrought-iron encased balcony. Directly below me was the hotel garden with its fountain, and pine and frangipani trees and a patch of lawn that was being swept by an old man wielding a witch's broom.

The room had all the necessary, if Spartan, mod cons including a TV. But the English channel was pitched so low I could not hear it. I wondered if this had been done on purpose. A nice touch though was that every day two pieces of fruit were added to the bowl on the table beside the bed. There was also a thermos for drinking water in my room. I filled it from a water container on a stand in the corridor but it absolutely refused to give the water back. There was no way the spout could be opened. The thermos seemed to be only for decoration, like some of the cupboard doors and drawers that didn't open and were only for show. The ones that did open didn't shut properly. They had a rough, hand-hewn look about them. And there was a cupboard I thought strange to find in a hotel room. It had a sloped front with a glass drop-down lid like an old baker's cake display unit. In it was enshrined, on view like the national treasure, a pretty ordinary plate, knife and two glasses. The bedside cupboards were immovable and apparently nailed to the floor. Inside the wardrobe the massive wooden coat hangers were permanently fixed to the rail. As if you'd want to stuff your bag with big lumps of tree – highly unlikely unless your kleptomania was out of control.

Fascinated by this relic of a hotel, I surreptitiously explored it. Near my room, in a large alcove hemmed all around with windows, was a sitting area containing a suite that consisted of an enormous carved wooden settee, four great armchairs, and a table. Truly the most hideous set of furniture ever made, it was flaunted in a manner to suggest that it was the pride of the management. I never saw anyone brave enough to actually sit on it.

The top floor, the sixth, was called the 'ballroom',

though how you could dance on the wall-to-wall carpet that covered it entirely escaped me. It was stupendously big; probably a small airport could have fitted in there. The runway would have been the room opposite it – another ballroom. This place must have been the meeting place for the all the communists in Asia, if not the world.

That night, tired after the long bus ride and my exploration of the massive hotel, I ate dinner at a nearby Indian restaurant and declared the day over early. Lying in bed with the curtains open I watched an amazing storm. Every few seconds the entire expanse of black sky in front of me was lit with a massive burst of sheet lightning. For a moment the outline of the riverside trees would be etched black against a dazzling white light. Thunderclaps, like the end of the world had come, followed each flash. I waited for the rain to begin but it didn't, it was a dry storm. Slowly the lightning flashes became fainter and fainter as the storm moved away, across the river and off to Thailand, decreasing in intensity as it went. At the height of the storm I had heard a plane take off. Nice. That's why I put up with the discomfort of buses.

Never one to miss breakfast, especially when it is free, I fronted early next morning eager to see what this would provide. The hotel's ground floor restaurant was the size of three football ovals and required a most intimidating walk across it, under the curious eyes of a platoon of staff, to get to where the food was. There, several big circular tables waited, girdled with bows and festooned with frills, reminiscent of restaurants in China.

The meal was rather good, if strange to Western taste. There was fruit, bread and juice and all sorts of Asian dishes including soup as well as eggs, ham, salad and condiments – all laid out for self-service on three big round tables. On my second morning I was joined at my table by a couple of men from an Asian delegation that was currently in town. One man, who started long after me, set to with a will to demolish a plate piled as high as an elephant's eye. He slurped, shovelled and champed through it like a threshing machine, and finished long before I did. I am no slouch at clearing my plate, but he beat me flat – and using chopsticks.

I set off to look for a bus going south to Pakse in a few days. It was Sunday and many offices were shut, but I did learn that if I wanted a comfortable air-conditioned bus I had to travel at night. Then I found one place open where a woman showed me a photo of the night bus. It looked diabolical. Being top-heavy double-decker buses driven fast by an often-fatigued driver, these contraptions are notoriously accident-prone. Once, years ago in Indonesia, I had travelled on one of these so-called 'sleeper buses'; it does not linger in my mind as the most enjoyable of experiences. I was reluctant to repeat it. Sleeper buses have no seats, just rows of narrow benches you lie down on, stacked like sardines, sleep looking to be the last thing possible.

The weather that day was oppressively hot and almost unbearably sticky. Sweat ran down my arms. I stopped to rest under a spreading tree in the grounds of a temple I was shortcutting through. A middle-aged Lao man approached and asked if he could share the seat with me. Then he said, 'Could I ask you a question?' He carried a sheaf of papers which he presented to me. I ended up doing his English homework for him. I hope he got an A or I am forever disgraced. The assignment was an interesting multi-choice questionnaire on the use of colloquialism. Try explaining what 'in the pink' means when asked 'why pink?' After we had finished he hailed a tuk tuk for me and saw me safely on my way to Talat Sao, the market, my next port of call. The card he gave me said that he was a pharmacist.

12 Goldfinger

The market was packed. It was Sunday and there were families everywhere. I looked for the young woman from whom I had bought the gold necklace when I had been there before. It was not easy finding her again; there were so many gold sellers in the old market, which is a veritable ant's nest of tiny shops.

On my previous visit she had told me that there were goldsmiths who did repairs here, and this time I had brought a job for them. Finally I located her and she directed me to the market's outer rim where these artisans sat on wooden stools, beavering away.

Each man had a tiny space allocated to him. It was fronted by a tatty wooden bench on which stood the accoutrements of his trade, a collection of old glass jars partly filled with various mysterious liquids, several tin bowls and miscellaneous clutter. I called them the Gnomes of Zurich although I am sure those other gnomes have very different working conditions. I showed the piece I wanted mended to a couple of the goldsmiths and was directed to a man who must have been considered capable of this task. He and I agreed to a price and I took a seat on one of the narrow wooden benches in front of the stalls as I had seen other women do when waiting for their mending.

Between the goldsmiths' benches and the market proper was a wide walkway, in which could be observed a fascinating insight into local life. I had plenty of time to do so; this was no rush job. The area was roughly roofed overhead, partly with sections of once wonderful embossed pressed tin, then with a collection of any old sort of tin or sacking, sections of which were falling down in places. It was extremely hot but I was pleased to see that my worker had a small electric fan.

A few metres from me, one of the market security guards was being fed his lunch. An itinerant food seller arrived, plonked down one six-inch-high plastic stool for him and another for herself, and proceeded to victualise him from items she dredged up from her bag and emptied into his bowl. He ate and then paid her what looked like one thousand kip, twelve cents. The goldsmith workers had home delivery of their meals too. I watched a girl came along collecting their empty bowls and their payment.

Meanwhile at the next stall, three men watched by an excited group of spectators gambled on a card game. Others further on played dominoes.

This area where the stalls end was where, towards the end of the day's trading, the rubbish was brought. Boxes of it were being dumped on the asphalt of the walkway. Soon an impossibly dilapidated hand-pushed cart came along, the pusher of which carried a witch's broom sweeper and a dustpan made from a cut-down kerosene tin stuck on a broom handle. He swept up the rubbish, then with his bare hands sorted it. He collected the cups that the fruit shakes and soft drinks had been sold in and stacked them up – for recycling, I hoped, not reuse.

A girl came to sit on the bench in front of the goldsmith next to mine. She handed him a gold earring and a five thousand kip note, seventy cents, and he soldered on the back of the earring. My job was more complicated. It took over an hour to replace a section of chain and repair two breaks in a necklace of gold beads. This smooth-faced, smiling Lao man worked a foot pump connected to a gas bottle to make a welding flame, and did all sorts of complicated things with the bottles and solutions on his bench. He then polished and revitalised my necklace back to better than new. The work was painstakingly carried out and a wonderful job. I was tremendously pleased.

The tuk tuk I rode back in for a rest before dinner cost more without my former friend, the pharmacist, to negotiate. You meet few people here who speak English, which sometimes makes getting around a bit difficult. *Oceans 13* was on the TV and I tried to watch it but it was hard to follow without sound. I waited until after dark to go out, hoping it would be cooler then. It was, and it had started to rain again.

In the street behind the hotel I found Vientiane's one small supermarket that sold western food. I stocked up on cheese, wholemeal bread and some Dutch cocoa in a terrific little tin. There I met the Irish girl and her boyfriend again. This is a place that westerners gravitate to in search of emergency supplies. It is near the city's main square, which has an impressive fountain in its centre. But in line with the government's curfew and their opinion that everyone should be home behaving themselves after dark, the water, along with most of the shops, shuts at eight pm.

Next morning I was homeless again, evicted into the street. After two days at the Lane Xang Hotel I was told I had to leave. The rooms had all been booked for an Asian conference. Lots of international heavies were expected and all the better hotels had no vacancies. I didn't mind. I had decided that I could do better than the LX, although by this time I had managed to get on friendly terms with the staff. Or, rather, they had overcome their reluctance to hobnob with a rarity such as me. I got the impression that few western travellers stayed there.

I phoned the Asian Pavilion. They were full too, but they promised me a room the day after next. I think. I was never sure. The phone connections are not good and the comprehension on both ends of the phone is worse. I got better phone reception when I called Australia. Not to mention comprehension. However, the Nalanthne Guesthouse took me in for the interim day.

This day was not my most illustrious. First eviction, then financial woes. The Lane Xang hotel rates were quoted in US dollars but I paid my bill in baht, allowing the receptionist to convert it to dollars. This was a big mistake. Do not do this. When I did my calculations and realised I had lost half my money in the hotel's conversion rate, I returned to the receptionist and discussed this with her. She obligingly gave me back my baht and let me pay with dollars. The moral of this tale is, carry the three currencies and pay with whichever is quoted.

I tuk tuked to check out Vientiane's other market. This is a sizeable place, with fruit, meat and fish so live they were flapping in the pans of water. And there were huge aluminum bowls of rice piled extraordinarily neatly into conical peaks. I saw two beggars here. One, a very old woman, sat on the floor of the walkway beside the produce; the other, a crippled girl whose legs appeared to have been blown off by a land mine, sat further along. I gave to both. I had bought a small tub of yoghurt for five thousand kip, an astronomical price by local standards, and thought that it was only fair that they should have at least the same amount of money.

The produce stalls ringed the extremity of the market, and the interior's hot, crammed aisles had what seemed like hundreds of tiny clothing stalls. There was a vast amount of stuff but most stalls seemed to have the same gear. I wondered how many made a sale each day. Some women stallholders whiled away the empty hours playing cards or dominoes on tiny tables. It was uncomfortable walking through this area; there was barely room to squeeze through between stalls. I wondered why I could smell a faint odour of ammonia until I realised that the rough concrete slabs, separated by gaping holes that ran along the centre of the walkway, covered a sewerage drain.

This day, hot and sunny, was another day waiting for rain, which came with a flash and a bang after dark when I ventured, totally smothered and almost gassed with insect repellent, to the Nalanthne's riverside restaurant for dinner. Memories of the bites I had sustained on this riverbank lingered. The waiter this evening was a 'ladyboy' who had a beautiful face and body but was too strong-looking to be a real Lao girl. This and the deep voice gave him away. No matter how I try not to, I find ladyboys intimidating. They make a parody of femininity that seems threatening to me, as though they are challenging me to do better. Am I revealing my deep-seated insecurities here? Probably.

During dinner I became aware of a faint, deep-voiced rhythmic chant, like someone counting off numbers. It grew and grew until it was quite loud, and then it became apparent that the sound was that of a dragon boat team approaching on the river. I hung over the restaurant railing to peer upriver in the direction of the chanting. Out of the gloom the boat emerged, then passed by. Forty men paddling as one, each stroke accompanied by a resonant chant, powered along an elongated, skinny boat that sat low in the water. It was quite a sight.

The room I had now in the Nalanthne was on the side of the building from where I could see the ongoing construction of an upmarket hotel next door. Workmen moved all over it on bamboo scaffolding of intricate design, two walking about on the very top without harnesses. I wondered how safe this was.

At breakfast I talked to an Australian woman who was in Laos for an extended stay and hoping to work for a charity organisation. We lingered in the dining room for a long time. I suppose I was starved for English conversation. Then I packed up and moved on, sharing a tuk tuk with her to the Asian Pavilion.

I was greeted warmly and ushered into the Asian Suite, no less. This was not the twenty-dollar-a-night single I had booked, but I was assured that for me it was the same price.

After a while I had the feeling I was not alone in this room. The clothes hanging in the wardrobe were the first hint. Just then the receptionist arrived, all of a fluster, to tell me he had made a mistake. I was still in the Asian Suite, but the other one on the opposite side of the corridor.

Later the receptionist gave me the welcome news that this room also included breakfast. Suits me. It turned out to be a voucher for use in the sidewalk cafe, and I could choose from a decent menu that included eggs. None of the hotel staff had more than a couple of words of English, but we communicated perfectly adequately most of the time with smiles and nods and pantomime.

The two Asian Suites encompass the entire front of the hotel's second floor and face the street. They were big enough to host a party, and I'll bet they saw a few in their day. From the wooden casement windows I had a good view of the street below. It was not very busy and the noise stopped at night, like everything else for that matter. The curfew of eleven helped. It was strange lying in bed in the gloom of the light from the street light, looking around this huge room, which took up about half the area of my small house back home. I had gone from a room in the Nalanthne

Guesthouse that managed to squeeze in a double bed with a three-foot clearance around it, to one that required hiking boots to make it to the bathroom. It's not often that I get a room within my budget that you can actually walk across.

When the two small side lights behind their delicately carved wooden shades over the dressing table were on, this room looked as if it once may have been quite swish. The cream-painted bamboo furniture, the red carpet, the pale-blue, shiny satin, once-expensive curtains and bedspreads on the twin double beds would have been top drawer in 1960. I could imagine this being the classy suite of the grand hotel that it once was. But in the cold light of day the fabrics were old, the carpet was torn and frayed, the wallpaper was patchy and the paint tatty. But for me the room was very comfortable. I no complain!

This hotel also exhibited a list of no-noes on the room wall. But on the same line as gambling and prostitution was a prohibition on 'cloth washing'. I often read similar threats of dire consequences for washing one's clothes in hotels. What's the big deal? Is it because they get commission from the laundry? Don't they want us to be nice, clean tourists? Despite the warnings, I always indulge in surreptitious, highly deviant and illegal washing. But I perform this secret vice guiltily. In my Asian Suite I ran into a problem.

The handbasin plug was one of those metal items that you open and close via a lever. I washed away happily and had the large tub full of dirty soapy water before I realised that the lever was broken – not an unusual occurrence for hotels past their prime – and I couldn't raise the plug to empty out the water. I used my scissors, then my screwdriver – yes, I never travel without my trusty screwdriver – but to no avail. Panic set in. How could I explain away the obvious evidence of my guilt? Would I be hauled away for 'education'? I bailed as much of the water as I could into the loo with my drinking glass. Sometime later I found a knife that, much to my relief, did the trick. But I steered well clear of that plug afterwards. I was not cured of the sin of washing; I just did it thereafter under a running tap.

It was a shame the days when spies frequented this hotel were over. I kept hoping to see a few. Now the clientele were mostly Asian tourists and it was a rather dull place. At least it wasn't full of backpackers. I was steering clear of them after the lot I saw in Luang Prabang, most of whom, except some of the older ones, were a disgrace.

I tried the Asian Pavilion's restaurant for lunch. It was cheap but westernised, the menu dwelling heavily on chips and hamburgers.

13 The common bus

Walking down the street to orientate myself to the area around the Asian Pavilion, I discovered that the other end of it finishes not far from the Lane Xang Hotel and the riverfront. Close by I found a woman in a shop who said she could organise me onto a bus that was not a sleeper. I decided to take this, the 'common bus' as she called it, to Tha Khaek, a sleepy riverside town some three hundred and thirty kilometres away and about halfway to Pakse, the last big town in the south. I planned to get to Pakse eventually and from there head down as far south as I could.

That this bus went to Tha Khaek was as much as I could find out. How to proceed any further was shrouded in mystery. I was to discover that this is generally the case – until you get to a place, you can't find out much about onward travel. All I gleaned from the many sources I enquired at was that it was possible to go further from Tha Khaek, but no one could agree on the details. Everyone gave me a different answer. Some gave several highly inventive versions. If I asked the question a second time, the story changed. I decided to take my chances. Anything is better than a night on a bus, thanks.

When first I entered the shop the proprietor had been taking her siesta on the floor of a room behind the counter. I had to wait several minutes for her to surface. I noticed that shops were often left unattended. Was this because most people are honest? Only in the western-orientated supermarket did I see spies snooping about in case someone swiped something. But even they were helpful if you wanted to know the price of an unlabelled item.

I needed to extend my month's visa before I left the capital. It cannot be done further south and I did not want to get into trouble at a border crossing again. I was a reformed character now.

I rode a tuk tuk to the Immigration Department office where I found a large hall, empty except for a row of uniformed officers sitting idly behind glass partitions – despite a surfeit of wooden benches and seats making it look like they were expecting a mob. Most tourists pay an agent to get their visa extensions for them but not me; I wanted to do it the hard way!

The form I had to complete cost me twenty-four cents. It was very inquisitive. It asked me why I was applying for an extension. I told the truth – for once. (I am not always truthful on forms if I think it's none of their business.) But now I said that Laos was so beautiful I needed more time to enjoy it. A bit of crawling never hurts, and I was dealing with a lot of uniforms behind those intimidating glass cages. Uniforms tend to make me extra nervous in a communist country. I have found they can mean serious trouble.

I took my completed form and passport down the line to uniform number 4 and while he was scrutinising it I read the notice that was stuck on the glass in front of me. It said that the fee for extension or fine for overstaying a visa did not apply to the following –

People over 65
People under 15

Disable people
Monks
Insane people

The latter tickled my funny bone and I had the urge to giggle. It seemed extremely strange to me that the Lao government would allow me to extend my stay for free if I would confess to being not the full quid. Or was this supreme kindness? Whatever, watching the gent in front of me who had more gold stars on his epaulets than the flag of the USA, I decided that sniggering was not a good idea. But it was hard to stop. I put my head down and fossicked in my bag as cover. Perhaps if I had giggled I might have got a free visa on the grounds of insanity anyway.

The star-spangled gentleman told me to come back at two and when I did it was a piece of cake to pay a couple of dollars and collect my new visa. Not so hard after all.

I set off then to follow the guidebook's recommended walking tour. First on the list was the Tourist Office, which was not far down the street I was in. This was a big surprise. Not the small, hopelessly inadequate place I had expected, it was big and spacious and well set out. You could watch videos of the various provinces and there were large wall charts and pamphlets available. I sat down to watch a video and have a rest in the lovely cool air-conditioning.

Then it was on to Wat Si Saket. Surrounded by a low line of monks' quarters built of wattle and daub, as well as a colonnaded terrace, it is said to be Vientiane's oldest surviving temple. At the gate I paid an admission fee of 5000 kip – locals pay 2000 (twenty-five cents) – and made my way along the terrace under the overhanging five-tiered roof, passing many large Buddha statues and the colourful scenes of the Buddha's life that are painted on the walls behind them. A high, wide flight of steps took me up to the temple building, and, at the top, divesting myself of my shoes, I moved inside.

A large gilded Buddha surrounded by more of the same dominated the interior. One of these companion statues was a thirteenth century Buddha seated on a coiled cobra with many *naga* heads curving protectively over his head. But the walls, or rather their contents, were the main feature of this temple. They were completely covered with row after row of small niches that proceeded all the way up to the roof and in each niche reposed a little Buddha statue. In total there were over seven thousand Buddhas in this temple. Before the temple was looted in the various wars that Laos has endured, the Buddhas in these niches were all solid gold or gilded, but now they are only clay.

Next on the tour list was the Haw Pha Kaeo. This was once a royal temple, built in 1565 to house the emerald Buddha, but is now the national museum of religious art. The emerald Buddha – which is not emerald, but jade – was captured and removed to Bangkok by the Thais in 1779 during one of their wars with Laos.

This was a huge place. Situated in lovely gardens and grounds, its wide set of steps that lead up to the temple – wats, being holy places, are always placed way up high – are guarded by two giant grey-bronze *naga* that slither gracefully up each side of them. At the top of the steps, one either side, stand two bronze life-sized Buddhas, and on the broad verandah surrounding the building were more – stone Buddhas dating from the sixth to the ninth century as well as several bronze standing and sitting Buddhas.

Most of the other visitors at these places of religious significance were tourists or pilgrims from surrounding Asian countries, predominately Thailand, who had come 'to sit at the feet of the Buddha', where they made offerings and paid homage. Reaching the two bronze guardian

Buddhas they rubbed their hands over the statues then over their own heads and chests. Further along the verandah was another large bronze Buddha, a beautiful, Lao-style, tall and lithe seventeenth-century one. This was the one I made reverence to – the Buddha known as Buddha Calling for Rain. He is always depicted standing upright with his arms straight down beside his body, his fingers open and pointing at the ground. Once I learned which Buddha was the rainmaker I made offerings to him whenever I found him, hoping he worked in Australia too. He certainly had been busy in Laos – there had been lots of rain.

On the temple steps a Thai girl asked if I would be photographed with her. Why, I pondered, would you want to spoil your holiday album with the inclusion of a frowsy, bedraggled stranger – and a decidedly strange stranger at that. On this baking, steamy day I even had sweat pouring down my face. Never mind the old adage that horses sweat, gentlemen perspire, but ladies glow. I had long since past the glow, moved through perspire, and was well and truly sweating like a cart horse – and probably smelling like one too.

Leaving the Haw Pha Kaeo I continued following the walking tour's directions, and, shaded by the spreading trees of Setthathirat Street, I should supposedly have arrived at the river. I did not. Eventually I found the river but I was nowhere near where I should have been. On my detour I passed the large, very European-looking Catholic church. It was white-painted with a high-peaked blue roof and bell tower, and looked like Dutch churches I had seen photos of.

Following the river I walked a long way but I seemed to be getting no closer to the centre of town where, according to the book, I should have been by now. But I did find Vientiane's wonderful long riverside promenade of ancient trees – massive teaks at least two hundred years old and enormous banyans. I stopped to worship their venerable gnarled trunks. Presently I met another lost tourist coming from the other end of the promenade, an English girl who seemed to have even less idea of where she was than I did. From our pooled knowledge we decided that we were both going in the wrong direction. A reversal was in order.

But I know when to give up on a hopeless cause. I hailed a tuk tuk and returned to the Asian Pavilion to lunch in my room on the wholemeal bread, cheese and yoghurt I had bought the night before in the supermarket in the square. Then I needed a rest. The heat was debilitating.

Later I walked again to the river. I was determined to see where I had gone wrong that morning. I am still not sure but I think I may have been heading in the right direction, just the long way round. Following the wall along the extensive grounds of the presidential palace, a big white stone construction that goes on forever, I passed 'The Economic Police Department'. I wondered if they were so named because they were cheap to run or whether they pursued you for your fiscal sins.

14 The case of the missing airport

After a couple of nights in the Asian Suite I no longer felt lost in its enormity. This particular morning I looked down into the street below, lined by small, narrow two-and three-storied shop houses, and saw that the asphalt of the road was wet. There had been more rain in the night, but it had not been enough to cool the day.

After breakfast I went off to the Talat Sao market again. It was time for some restoration work. I needed hair help. Having checked out the price of hair colouring at the only hairdresser I found and learned that it cost 300,000 kip, I opted to do it myself. This must be an exotic and rare procedure in Laos to cost so much when an hour of intense massage could be had for 4000 kip. I knew from past attempts in Asian countries that DIY hair interference is not necessarily wise unless you want to come out with jet-black tresses. I had tried this colour once and ended up looking as if all I needed to complete the picture was a lamppost to lean on. There was another option, however, according to a sign outside the hairdressers that offered:

Pull out white Hares

Well, that's one way I suppose.

Finally, one Madame in the market, who presided over a stall devoted to female fittings, helped me decipher the packets and select something that may or may not be near my colour.

Moving on, I bought a replacement umbrella, pink of course. My current brolly had been getting more and more debilitated by the day, until finally it had given up the ghost. Now I sported Pink Umbrella Mark 2. I hoped this one would go the distance. My one pair of shoes were not travelling well either. I don't imagine Nina Ferrari had riding elephants, falling in the mud and being hosed down in mind when she had made those shoes. They were limping badly.

Another errand was to return to the stall where I had bought my previous phone card, where the same young man put another card into my phone for me.

It was very hot in the non-air-conditioned old part of the market, but I wandered happily there for hours in its maze of tiny stalls before walking back to the Asian Pavilion. Now that I had my bearings I had discovered that the market was not far from there.

Two hours of rest later I was off again, this time to complete the last three tourist imperatives in Vientiane. The tuk tuk rider, a good-natured lad who had a regular spot outside the Asian Pavilion and who had become my usual choice of transport, took me there and back. I was flagging and wanted no more walking in this town.

My first stop, in central Vientiane, was the Lao National Museum. It resided in a 1920s building that was formerly the colonial police commissioner's office. Large parts of the museum's exhibits leaned heavily towards glorifying the revolutionary Pathet Lao's struggle for liberation, but there were also interesting displays relating to Lao royalty and the colonial years. The highlight for me were the artifacts from the country's fifty main ethnic groups such as musical instruments and handcrafts.

Not far from the centre of the city was the next attraction on my list, the rather wonderful arch, Patuxai. A Lao version of Paris's Arc de Triomphe, it dominates a wide boulevard much in the manner of the French original. It is referred to by some irreverent local wits as the 'vertical runway' because it was meant to be an airport! (An easy mistake to make.) In 1960 the USA gave Laos the cement to build an airport. The Lao, very sensibly, built a decorative arch instead. As you do. It is a thing of beauty, as an airport never can be. It stands imposingly, straddling the road at the head of a broad, sweeping stretch of avenue, doing its best to look as Gallic as possible. You can climb to the top of the arch for a panoramic view of the city, but there is no merit attached to this feat so I was content to just stand inside it looking up at the colourful decoration of the interior. Across the roof of the arch's underside are beautiful vivid paintings and mosaics. Behind the arch is a large green park with a big, high-flying musical fountain, a gift from the Chinese.

A further four kilometres on is Pha That Luang (Great Reliquary), Lao's most important national monument. This large golden stupa is both a symbol of the Buddhist religion and of the Lao people's freedom and independence. Its full name means World-Precious Sacred Stupa. The present structure's construction began in the middle of the 16th century when King Setthathirat moved the capital of Laos from Luang Prabang to Vientiane. The stupa was built on the site of a Khmer temple that existed here between the eleventh and thirteenth centuries, which in turn was said to have been placed on the site of a reliquary stupa put there around 300 BC by missionaries from India to house part of the breastbone of the Buddha. Or to guard a hair of the Buddha, depending on whose account you read.

The stupa is massive. I could see its gilded forty-five

metre height glittering heavenwards from a long way off as the tuk tuk rattled up to it. Its shape represents the growth of a lotus from seed to bloom – and the growth of humanity from ignorance to enlightenment through Buddhism.

The approach to the monument was lined on one side (but at least far away in the background) with low humpies of stalls loaded with tourist clobber. Passing these, I arrived at the entrance gate where old or crippled sellers offered the merit-producing small birds in bamboo cages for do-gooders to release. I hoped that the poor birds that weren't sold that day would be given food and drink. They must get very hot sitting there all day in the sun.

Inside the gate and in front of the monument is a statue of King Sitthathirat, seated on a throne and wearing a remarkable piece of headwear – a cross between a pith helmet and a conquistador's hat. Two flags fly above him, the blue and red Lao national flag, and the Communistic red flag with the yellow hammer and sickle that usually accompanies it.

I walked around the extensive square at the base of the stupa that is surrounded by a high-walled cloister and contains stone statues of the Buddha. Steps ascend to three levels. On the third, thirty golden pinnacles encircle the stupa. The complex grounds cover several acres and are flanked by two big beautiful temples with a predominance of curved and sweeping roofs and much gilding. From one of these temples came the rhythmic chanting of male voices. Dark, purple-black rain clouds were gathering behind the temple roofs, and the contrast of the golden sweeps and curves of the roof against the clouds was simply stunning. But I longed for these clouds to produce some rain. The sky had spotted a drop or two off and on all day but a great monsoonal downpour was what was needed to relieve the heat.

Pha That Luang is another holy place of pilgrimage, and as at others I visited, I saw only a couple of other westerners. The Asian sightseers prayed, making offerings of marigolds and incense.

That night I ate dinner at the Blue Banana, a cafe a short distance up the street from my hotel where the fruit shake I ordered came served in a glass so tall I either had to stand up to get above it or put it in my lap. I had some trouble getting a cup of black coffee here – this did not feature on the menu and after much consultation among the staff I was told, 'No have'.

So I said, 'Like breakfast.' It worked!

I ordered 'Steak smashed style with beautiful'; which turned out to be the ubiquitous *laap*. It was a perfectly correct translation – the meat was smashed and it was beautiful.

Accustomed now to my Asian Suite, when the time came to leave it the next day I didn't want to, wondering what might lie ahead for me as I headed south to less touristed places. But I was glad I did because Tha Khaek turned out to be the best place I had found so far. It felt like the real Laos, nor some trumped-up place for tourists to gawk at. I know I am a tourist and I gawk as much as the rest of them, if not more, but …

The bus ticket I had bought included pickup from my hotel. It wasn't due to arrive until midday so, deciding that a relaxing dose of reflexology might set me up for the travels ahead, I repaired across the road to such an establishment. Here, in a darkened atmospheric room, a young girl inflicted as much pain on me as anyone could possibly need. Reflexology's claim is that each area of your foot is connected to some part of your body, and a place on your foot that hurts when pressed means that the corresponding part of your body is not well. Massaging this spot until it stops hurting is supposed to fix what ails you. Well, from the excruciating pain in every bit of my foot into which this small operator dug her amazingly strong little fingers, it was painfully obvious that all my bodily organs were in a state of imminent collapse. Hopefully, though, they were now in the process of being cured as I gritted my teeth and bore the torture with true valour.

But when my tormentor produced a pointed wooden stick the size of a chair leg and indicated that she wanted my consent to use it on me, I faltered. Images of all manner of nasty oriental practices flashed before my eyes. The reality was almost as bad. The smiling assassin dug this object into all my toe joints in succession, watching me to see how much it hurt. Yelping and jumping out of the chair was what I wanted to do but I was brave and told myself it was good for me. I came out of the building feeling terrific, mainly because it was over and I had been released.

At noon I sat waiting in the hotel lobby as ordered by the bus people. I was still waiting at half past when the waiter from the restaurant, the one person who spoke some English, fortuitously strolled by. Before, whenever panto-mime communication efforts between the receptionists and me had failed, one of them would go next door to the res-taurant and find him. Now he phoned the bus ticket people who should have collected me. They said they were coming. Ten minutes later, there was still no sign of my transport and the bus departure time was rapidly approaching. The waiter phoned again.

Finally something arrived, not a tuk tuk but a tiny moped, and no matter how the rider tried he could not fit my bag, my handbag and me on this tin-pot toy. It was hopeless. Now the moped rider phoned the company. I was in a tizzy. It was almost lift-off time for the bus, and the bus station was at least twenty minutes away. Finally, at seven minutes to bus time a van arrived. 'The bus wait you at stoplight,' its driver announced, shoveling me in.

He then proceeded to fly down the road and out of town. After we ran the second red light at speeds of one hundred kilometres an hour among traffic, that, thank goodness, was sparse, I stopped looking. A scream of brakes jolted my eyes back to the road in time to see the back of a truck a few inches from my face. Ten kilometres from the edge of the city the bus sat waiting, as promised, at a crossroads. Thankfully, I clambered on under the critical eyes of the passengers I had kept sitting in the sun. How embarrassment, as Effie would say.

My reserved seat was occupied. Reservations do not hold good for latecomers I gathered, so I stumbled to the back of the bus where a four-person bench stretched across from side to side. One man sat on either end and I asked permission to sit between them. This was a good position. It gave me plenty of space to stretch my legs into the aisle in front of me. The window seats either end of the bench had cup rests and a shelf and a wide space in front of them. Very deluxe. It took me two hours to work out that I had intruded on passengers who had paid extra for these privileged seats. As usual with the polite Lao, these gentlemen were too nice to refuse me. One spoke English well. He said he was going to work at Savannakhet, two hours further on from Tha Khaek. He was a cabinetmaker and the young man on the other end of the seat was his apprentice. After a while he asked my permission to put his feet up on the shelf, then covered them with a blanket, offered me one too, and settled down to sleep. If I hadn't been there he would probably have stretched out across where I now sat.

This bus only went as far as Tha Khaek. He had to change buses there for Savannakhet and he had a long journey ahead.

The narrow road took us through the usual green countryside. Sometimes there was flat land with rice paddies and at other times we were among hills covered in dense forest devoid of habitation. The villages I saw were small and simple. Southern Laos is quite different from the north of the country. Unlike the north, which for centuries has been isolated by its mountainous terrain, the broad Mekong valley, lowlands and high plateau of the south were accessible to farmers and traders from China and surrounding areas.

We stopped once for the nicotine addicts' fix at a rickety wooden-decked place. I took this stationary opportunity to use the bus loo. It was underneath the passenger seats down on the first level, used for freight and baggage, of the double-decker bus.

In Vientiane when I had enquired about travelling south by bus, all office personnel had insisted that the night bus was the only option, until I found the woman who had sold me the ticket on this bus, the 'common bus'. Anything but the horrors of a sleeper bus, I had thought as I bought a ticket.

A couple of hours out of Vientiane I thanked heaven that I had. Outside the window I saw a chilling sight. On its side, all smashed up in a ditch beside the road, lay the previous night's sleeper bus! Who says there is not an angel who looks after fools and innocents? There in that ditch, but for my own particular angel, would I have been.

An hour later we passed the scene of another accident – a car upside down in the ditch, also smashed up, with people milling around it.

I had it in writing on my ticket that this bus took four hours to reach Tha Khaek. It took six, arriving near seven in the evening. As it usually did, I was told. Communication between towns is poor. It was dark and raining heavily, as it had been for the past hour or so, when I stepped down from the bus. Parting company with my generous companion, he wished me a good journey as I commandeered a lurking tuk tuk.

A few backpackers climbed in with me. They had the usual issue about the fare with the driver, taking the matter far too seriously I considered. We drove around a good while before they decided on rooms and I could get rid of them and move on to the Southida Guesthouse where I had phoned for accommodation. A good thing about Lao tuk tuk drivers is that they don't try to up the ante when you arrive at your destination. When a price has been agreed, they stick to it.

Again I found that the guidebook's recommendations were not entirely to my taste. I had wisely avoided what they had said was the best budget place, knowing that it was probably a dump. It was. It was also, because of their advice, full. The Southida attendant showed me a couple of rooms and I chose one on the top floor. It had a marvellously strange shape and an amount of windows that were on the outer limit of excessive. Almost all wall space was window, five in the small room as well as a tiny Juliet balcony. The bathroom let the standard of the room down. Above all else I like a nice bathroom, and the VIP one of the Asian Suite had spoiled me. This toilet didn't even get rid of fluids. As for asking it to cope with toilet paper – forget it. The tiny bathroom was half filled by a big pink plastic drum of water and a dipper, fine for washing and essential for the recalcitrant toilet.

The room was a monument to woodcarving. The

enormous bed, the beautiful polished ceiling, paneled walls, cupboards, table and casement windows were all marvels – and solid. I tried to move a tiny side table and couldn't lift it off the floor. I think the wood was teak. It was certainly a hardwood of some kind. The floor was covered in shiny red tiles.

I enquired about food that night and was shown a breakfast menu. 'Now?' I asked hopefully. Breakfast is my favourite meal anytime of the day.

'Morning is all!' was the reply.

I prepared to bed down supperless, as there appeared to be no place to eat in the surrounding streets. Then I remembered the cheese and banana sandwich I had brought for the bus ride, which was still, thankfully, in my bag, although much sat and trodden on.

Then with an almighty clap of thunder the rain started to fall in earnest. Lovely, substantial, teaming rain bucketed down accompanied by almost constant thunder that sounded like someone rattling a sheet of corrugated iron overhead. Great flashes of lightning lit the room. The storm continued for most of the night, cooling the air so that I was able to turn off the air-conditioner, which was fortunate as its controls were fixed on frigid and no amount of coaxing could persuade them to change.

Breakfast may have been the only meal available at the Southida but it was a good, solid meal and after it next morning I went exploring.

15 Tha Khaek

Following the night of rain the morning was relatively cool. The Southida Guesthouse is in a small street that runs down to the Mekong, and soon I was walking along the river's edge under shady trees. Thailand was clearly visible on the other side of the river. Tha Khaek is a river port, a crossing point between Laos and Thailand, and freight boats and ferries were coming and going busily.

It didn't take me long to decide that I liked Tha Khaek. The riverside road was not very wide and almost no traffic came along it. Dotted under the trees on the bank were small local eating places and stalls selling drinks in bottles and cans as well as junk food in packets. Not the touristy cafes of Luang Prabang and Vientiane, but mere wooden benches and stands. No one pestered me to buy. The river scene was much more relaxed here.

Now and then along the edge of the river I came to rough-hewn steps in the riverbank that led down to small timber landings where wooden boats waited. Further on there was a floating restaurant. Merely a big pontoon with a roof, it looked like a fun place for mosquitoes and sand-flies. I reckoned they would be doing most of the dining there. So far I'd only collected one more bite – a beauty, two inches across – since the initial mess I'd been made of by the insects of Vientiane.

On the other side of the river road were houses and a

few small shops, in one of which I was served by a tiny four-year-old girl. We got on just fine. When your only method of communication is pantomime you are on the same level as a four year old anyway. Cruising along the shop's two wide, sparsely-filled shelves looking for some hand cream, eventually I found something that looked hopeful. Made in Thailand, it cost less than two dollars and promised anti-aging as well as vitamins. Having recently read in the Vientiane News that a company in Thailand had been prosecuted for selling cosmetic creams containing lead and horrible nasties like tetra carbonates, I hoped that this was not one of their products. Incidentally, I also read in that paper that twelve people had been sentenced to death in Vietnam for fraud – selling or making fake goods.

Further along the road curved around, left the river and looped back through the town. I kept walking and passed the 'square of the fountain', of which latter item there was no sight. Much building was happening in the square; perhaps the fountain was away for R and R. Around the square and the street behind the river road, which seemed to be the main part of town, some interesting old buildings remained from the days of French colonialism. Streaked with black tropical mould, they looked ancient. Some had been restored by the United Nations. Different from colonial architecture I had seen elsewhere, they had balconies on the upper levels and arched colonnades in front of their entrances.

Spotting a shop with a sign that said 'travel', I went in to see if they organised buses further south. A young man half my height took me smiling – are they ever anything else? – into an office where a lovely girl and another young man tried to help me. It turned out that this business only rented vehicles but they told me where to go (the polite version anyway) – the local Tourist Information Office.

I set off and was a little further along the street when the girl from the office came up behind me on a motorbike and offered me a ride. I accepted gladly. Although the morning had been cool it hadn't been long before the sun had the residue of the night's rain steaming.

Tha Khaek's Tourist Information Office lurks in a dark, wooden house set well back from the road a couple of kilometres from the centre of the town, not an entirely handy location, but I don't imagine they get a lot of business. I climbed the wide wooden steps up to the house and inside found maps and local information spread around the walls. After an epic struggle of mutual incomprehension with the office boy, the boss, who looked only slightly older but had a shirt and a tie, came out of a side office and took over. He convinced me that what I needed to do was take a tour the next day to visit the two features the district offered – the Caves of the Buddha and the Great Wall. They were both some distance away so it would take all day, he said.

I strolled slowly back to the Southida, stopping off on the way at a market the girl on the motorbike had pointed out to me as we rode past. She said that traders from Thailand come across the river to set up stalls there in an open paddock. I had to slosh about in mud and puddles and it wasn't a very interesting market from my point of view, mostly household items, bits and pieces of frippery for the hair and cheap jewellery. Not that I am adverse to a bit of frippery, it just wasn't my type. But I did buy a wide-toothed comb. They are not so easy to find in Adelaide.

The road I followed was the main road in or out of the town, but even on that the traffic was sparse and mostly two-wheeled. Men puffing cigarettes rode past me on motorbikes. Women sat on pillion seats and held umbrellas, tiny babies wrapped in shawls tied to their chests. Some riders also shaded themselves with umbrellas as they travelled along. Small children often were seated in front of the motorbike rider.

I heard a ting-ting ring behind me and turned to find its origin. There, stepping daintily down the middle of the road, her neck bell jingling musically, came a lovely velvety-brown nanny goat with her two little dark-brown kids trotting dutifully behind. Then I heard another unusual sound – a loud rendition of the Mexican Hat Dance. It was the horn of the vehicle that was the Lao version of Mr Whippy, a motorbike with a blue-painted sidecar containing an ice chest of frozen goodies. I supposed that as today was Saturday and the little dears were out of school, Mr Whippy figured they were free to pester their mums for ice-cream just like in any country of the world.

I came to a large wat whose grounds led through to the river, where I stopped to marvel at an enormous and simply stunning tree. Thank goodness Buddhists revere all living things, especially wonderful trees. Not only did the Lord Buddha receive enlightenment under a Bhodi tree but many of the Lao who became Buddhists retain the animistic belief that trees have spirits, as do I.

Next door to the wat on the riverfront was the Mekong Hotel, a massive electric blue pile four storeys high. It looked interesting, if only for its large expanse of startling colour. I ventured in to investigate. The prices were similar to the Southida's and I liked its position and ambience, not to mention the bathing facilities in the room I was given a tour of.

The Mekong's other attraction was a pleasantly positioned restaurant almost on the river. I had lunch there. The food was excellent and inexpensive, and the coffee was the real thing at sixty cents a big pot. The breeze off the water stirred the bead curtain that hung over the arches of the blue-painted (what else, I think they got a huge supply of this blue paint cheaply) wooden divider that was the restaurant's only separation from the riverbank road. Two large trees shaded its front and several big tubs of flowering plants flanked its sides. The tubs were decorated to the nth degree. Nothing is left to chance here. If something can be embellished or tarted up in any way, it will be. From where I sat to eat I could see the neighbouring wat and watch the monks in their orange and saffron robes moving about the grounds.

A siesta followed, and I set off again at six in the evening when the weather was cooler. Flagging down a tuk tuk, I discovered that there were already passengers aboard, but apparently this is no deterrent. In fact, having people as witnesses embarrasses the driver into giving you the local price. I was off to the main market, three kilometres or so away from the river area.

This market consisted mainly of food and clothes, and, judging by the attention I got, the most curious item there turned out to be me! I bought a shirt to eke out my meagre wardrobe but it took quite a time to find something big enough to fit me. My size was subjected to a lot of giggles and I began to feel enormous – a strange experience for skinny me.

After this lesson in humility, I galloped through the meat section with my mental nose peg on. I always think of my sister when I am in an Asian meat market. In all my years of nursing the only time I ever saw anyone actually turn green was when she had to walk through a meat market in Sumatra. If I hadn't hauled her out bodily I believe she would be there still, a crumpled heap on the floor.

In another section of this market I saw wide aluminum bowls that held small live brown frogs, not like the big frogs that the French eat but rather like the marsh frogs I was breeding at home (because I like the noise they make and they keep the mosquitoes down). There were also live crabs, snails and small silver fish flapping in shallow metal pans.

I decided that according to the guidebook map, although they are not always reliable, I should be able to walk to a nearby guesthouse where I could get dinner. After hiking what seemed a long way and not necessarily in the right direction, it started to rain. I scurried across the road to the only shelter in view, a verandah over a shop front. A group of men sitting at a table under it hailed me. I approached and asked directions. They appeared a trifle inebriated – not hard to deduce, it was Saturday night and there were a lot of beer bottles on their table. But they did know where I wanted to go. They said it was close and pointed the way. Remarkably, I had been on the right track.

The Tha Khaek Travel Lodge (not to be confused with, or in any shape or form having any resemblance to the famous worldwide motel chain except in name) turned out to be a welcoming place. As I approached it a French couple I had met when we had all been looking for bus tickets in Vientiane hailed me from one of the outdoor tables. I joined them and had a meal of green curry and rice. I had a spot of bother convincing the girl taking the order that I didn't have a room number. This seemed to mystify her. I wondered if they only fed their residents and I was going to be denied food. But in due course the curry arrived. Later, this young woman, the manager of the guest-house, returned and asked, 'Are you alone?' When I said yes she announced, 'Then I will take you home when you are ready.' I puzzled about this – young women taking me places on motorbikes. It happened to me several times in Lao and I could only presume that it was pure kindness. Or that I was such an oddity I warranted closer observation.

The French couple, Emile and Elise, and I had a good chat over dinner. She had excellent English and translated for him. They were great readers and we shared many favourite authors. Sitting under the verandah that covered the tables and watching the rain fall down into the dark night outside our circle of light was extremely satisfying.

When it came time to leave my new friend and I took to the saddle. She rode very carefully and slowly and there was little else on the road so we had a conversation as we went along. I asked her if she often ferried home stray visitors and she told me that she had never done it before. All the foreigners she met were staying in the guesthouse. She added naively that she did it because she liked the look of me. (The nose again?) I asked if she was married and she said, 'No,' adding, 'I would like to be but I am not beautiful.' This touched me greatly. It was one of the saddest things I have heard a young girl say. It shouldn't matter that she was indeed rather plain, but if she believed it then it did matter. Especially in a country like Lao that is absolutely bursting at the seams with beautiful girls. Hopping off at the Southida I promised to go back for another meal before I left.

Sarae had also told me that she worked seven days a week. Obviously there are no workers' unions in Lao. I learned that the poor boy who had been manning the desk at the Southida since I got there worked twenty-four hours around the clock, sleeping when he could.

I fell into bed, was asleep almost at once and had a full ten minutes slumber before loud shouting in the corridor outside my room rudely awakened me. It got worse. There were sounds of heavy furniture being dragged across tiled floors, music, singing and raucous laughter. Everyone was having a good time except me. I was not amused. The racket kept up until after three am and then I had a couple of hours of sleep.

In the morning, viewing the wreckage remaining in the

rooms of my floor, I deduced that the night's festivities had been a wedding. They could have warned me or at least invited me to join in. The fact that I checked out after breakfast may have enlightened the management to my lack of enthusiasm for a repeat of this performance.

I waited until the nice young man from the tourist office, he of the shirt and tie, came to collect the money for my day's outing, then I trundled my bag down the street, around the corner onto the riverside road and moved into the Mekong Hotel.

16 The long lunch

The spacious riverfront room I now had in the Big Blue Pile was only a dollar more than the Southida but the cons were far more mod. Outside my door, a wide shining-tiled balcony ran the length of the building and from it I could see the river traffic passing close by. Space was one item that had not been skimped on in the building of this hotel – everything was large scale – and there was a cool, open feeling to the place. From the sweeping expanse of the lobby, a wide staircase ascended to the broad verandah off which the rooms proceeded. In contrast to the Southida, which was all wood – heavy, solid staircases, handrails and panelled walls – the Mekong was painted concrete and tiles. Even the balustrades of the staircase were mammoth constructions of cement, painted blue of course.

At nine am a diminutive chap collected me. He was to be my guide for the day. I was sorry he wasn't the shirt and tie, who was not only better looking but also spoke a reasonable amount of English. It was very shortly established that this guide, Mei, and I scored poorly in the dialogue stakes. His weirdly accented English was as incomprehensible to me as mine was to him. After a while I realised that he did not understand English at all. He was only parroting a few phrases he had learned. I gave up. I liked Mei, he was a jolly person, but he had been fraudulently represented as an English-speaking guide.

We embarked on what was to become a gruelling six-hour day. And Mei originally had wanted to do it on a tiny motorbike. No thank you, I had said firmly, rejecting the proffered iron steed. He then phoned for back up and a friend arrived with a tuk tuk. Also, Mei's girlfriend, another tiny person, joined us. Both were named, Mei told me (I think), Noi.

It quickly became apparent that Mei saw our day's outing as an excuse for an eating fest for him and the two Nois. That the prodigious amount of food purchased this day would be blamed on my gluttony when the expense account went in was plain. First Mei stopped at a roadside vendor for baguettes. I politely refused one, not only because of the unhygienic appearance of the preparation bench but also because of the horrible-looking meat paste goo with which the maker was stuffing them.

Next we moved on to the market where to shut Mei up I let him buy several large portions of cooked food of indeterminate origin. Scooped up into plastic bags from where they had been sitting in open tin basins on the ground, they looked positively poisonous and I had no intention of eating any. You know I am not too precious when it comes to food but this was beyond the pale.

I made a stand, however, when it came to the frog kebabs. The sight of row after row of the poor little bodies flattened, skewered and barbecued on bamboo slivers was too much. He bought fish and pork kebabs and bananas and oranges instead.

A long ride through the countryside followed. The scenery was lovely. Karsts rose sharply out of the green land, heavily wooded except for occasional bare patches of a pale ochre colour romantically streaked with black. All the land, as far as I could see from the road, was water logged. The last few nights' torrential rains had caused the rivers that flowed through there to overflow. I saw huts with flood-waters right up to their roofs but no flooded houses. The local people are too savvy to build where inundation is likely; the flooded huts were only rice paddy shelters.

Men fished the waters with triangular nets on poles or with rods. Some were catching grasshoppers, which are fried and eaten. Animals wandered the sides of the road. The tan-coloured cows and calves were mostly skinny, consumptive-looking creatures with protruding ribs. They dragged along as though it was almost too much trouble to put one foot in front of the other. The cows appeared untended, but one of each group wore a bell and I guessed she was the oldest and most sensible whose job it was to lead the others home. In contrast the grey water buffalo, some wallowing happily up to their necks in water, were fat and sleek. Goats also ambled along the verge beside the road and plump white geese busily fossicked in the paddy fields.

Visits to two caves were on the agenda but on arrival at the stepping-off place for the first cave, Tham Xang (Elephant Cave), the path we were supposed to walk on was no more. Instead we found a broad expanse of water, caused by the overflow of the river that runs past it. Several villagers had just waded through this and they indicated to us that the water reached past their waists. These were the men, but I could see that the women were wet all the way up to their necks. Mei, determined to make me be a Good Little Tourist, urged me in. I told him no.

Clearly he had not thought this through. If the water came anywhere near my chest, his nose would be under-water! I don't mind getting wet when the weather is hot but this water was swirling and raging and goodness knows what snags lay underneath its murky depths. I baulked. We retreated.

Another long drive to the next cave, Tham Pha Pa (the Buddha Cave), ensued, and we stopped off on the way to visit a local market. Housed in a structure like a bough shed with a thatched roof, herbal cures and produce were displayed on wooden platforms. Mei bought corncobs that had been roasted on the coals of a brazier, ostensibly for me, even though I said I didn't want one. The other three enjoyed them however. I had lost my appetite at the sad sight of the little dead body of a beautiful animal that looked like a brush-tailed possum or a sugar glider (possibly endangered) and some very tatty rabbit corpses laid out among the vegetables and herbs. The living offerings were just as depressing, thoroughly miserable-looking chooks huddled in tiny bamboo containers or just lying dejectedly on the ground with their legs tied. Animal lovers should not visit Asian produce markets.

Moving on, I recovered. The country continued to be pretty, and when we did eventually reach the Buddha Cave it was well worth the ride. I was really impressed.

This cave was only recently discovered. A local hunter saw some bats fly from the limestone karst and, using a vine, he had scaled the two hundred metre sheer cliff face and found a cave opening. Stepping inside he met an astounding sight – hundreds of Buddha statues stared back at him! They sat serenely facing the entrance as they had for countless undisturbed centuries. Although their origins are long forgotten, they are estimated to have been left sitting there in peace for around six hundred years. This cave that kept its secret for aeons is now a holy pilgrimage site for Lao and Thai Buddhists.

But first Mei and the two Nois had their sights on more food. The usual way to reach the cave was via a path and over a bridge to the foot of the mountain that housed the cave, but now nothing was in sight except a wide sheet of water. On the high ground in front of this lake stood two long palm-thatched roofs that sheltered rows of low bamboo platforms covered with straw mats. Around the edges of the platforms several women manned food stands, cooking rice in clay pots or barbecuing kebab skewers on braziers filled with coals. Their customers sat cross-legged on the platforms to eat from dishes placed before them on the mat.

Mei, the Nois and I settled ourselves on a platform and the daylong pig-out continued. All the food Mei kept buying – allegedly for me – was not wasted. Those three scoffed continuously. Several times I said I didn't want any more rice but mountains of it kept coming. An awful lot of food that had been bought in my name went into those stomachs. What I did eat though, I enjoyed. The small fish barbecued on bamboo sticks in rows like kebabs were delicious. The pork done the same way in thin crispy pieces was good too. Then there was green pawpaw salad, bananas to finish, and water to drink. Small dogs came to share our meal and beg for the scraps.

To make it across the lake to the mountain now entailed a canoe ride. I wobbled down into one of these very flat craft, and, perilously close to sitting with my bottom in the water, was paddled slowly and languorously across the flat, green, algae-flecked water made dark by the shadow of the overhanging mountain. Roughly made wood and bamboo steps ascended the precipitous face of the mountain that had to be scaled to reach the cave. The steps were slippery with mould and algae and I proceeded gingerly. At the top of the steps a woman guardian sat on a small ledge. She gave me a sarong to cover my pants. You are not permitted to enter this holy place improperly dressed. I bought an offering, a bundle of incense sticks and fragrant white flowers like tuberoses, to atone for my sinfulness. Then, ducking under an overhanging ledge, I stepped cautiously through the narrow opening and, with some difficulty, found toeholds in the rock and descended steeply down into the interior cave.

Clutching my offering I stood and goggled, stunned. The cave is surreal. Two hundred and twenty nine Buddha statues, some tiny and some a metre tall, stand among great formations of ghostly, creamy-white stalactites and stalagmites. Illuminated only by the dim light of flickering candles, there was a truly religious feeling here, quite unlike the other Buddha cave I had visited in the north. I was the only tourist here; everyone else had come to pay reverence.

Behind this large cave, through a high dome-shaped entry, I could see another big cave. This second one is the most holy and visitors can only look into it, not enter.

In the first cave a few local people and pilgrims knelt praying. An old man and woman seemed to be the cave guardians. They lit my incense sticks and I knelt down, bowed three times and placed them and my flowers before the main altar. As usual I prayed for rain. Mei and Noi both made offerings and reverence. The old man gestured for me to sit in front of him, and, cross-legged on the floor of the cave, I received the *baci* ceremony – blessings to keep you safe as well as a welcome to country. The old man wiped up and down my arm with a saffron-coloured cord as he recited blessings. Then he tied the cord around my wrist. The old woman then did the same on my other arm and wrist. I got down from the cave unscathed, so the blessing must have worked. So far every now and then on the day's travels, Noi, Noi, Mei, or all three had had to shove and haul me in, up and out of the high back of the tuk tuk, so I figured I needed all the help I could get.

Climbing into a canoe waiting on the waters of the

dark-green pool at the mountain's base, I returned again to dry land. I had read that the local people eat the algae on the water, how I couldn't imagine. But I could see that there would be plenty to eat in the water that abounded across the countryside if you weren't too fussy – snails, frogs and grasshoppers, small fish and weeds.

A long ride back to the edge of the town brought us to the location of the district's other viewing must, the Great Wall. This intriguingly named object is part of an ancient city wall, the derivation of which has been lost in time. No one seemed to know when it was built. Reaching it required a hike into the surrounding forest, and coming upon it suddenly and unexpectedly, hidden deep and partly overgrown with clinging vines, was a surprise.

Close up the wall was massive. Three storeys high and built of stupendously big blocks, each the size of a Volkswagen, one on top of the other, it continues for fifteen kilometres. A lost, rather mysterious feeling pervaded this silent place.

I would have been perfectly content to stand and admire the wall from afar but my captors were determined to make me continue being a Good Little Tourist. They forced me to climb up and over the structure using toeholds in the rock face, pushing and hauling me when I flagged.

As I tramped back to the tuk tuk through the forest on the other side of the wall, strange spiders with tiny bodies and long skinny legs ran away from my approaching feet and Mei showed me a toad, a fine, fat fellow sitting in the mouth of his hole in the ground. I would not have seen him. Motionless and the same colour as the leaf litter on the ground, he was well camouflaged.

But still I was not released from the bondage I had entered into with these two tiny people and their accomplice. I had to endure more of the tuk tuk, jolting a further six kilometres back to the other side of the town to view a sixteenth-century temple, Pha That Sikhottabong, a much-venerated place. Built originally on the site of a reliquary stupa dating from the sixth to the tenth centuries, it now stands in the peaceful gardens of a nineteenth-century monastery. Crossing an ornamental bridge over a stream, I visited the large central hall and paid my respects to a huge gilded sitting Buddha.

I paused at this stage to wonder how Siddhartha Gautama, the Lord Buddha, feels about all this worship. I secretly believe he would be as appalled as Jesus to see what is done now in his name. I don't imagine either of them set out to be worshipped. And all the money these poor people spend on offerings to him! It's OK to feed monks but stray dogs and birds eat most food offerings.

Finally released after six hours of performing my sightseer act, I retired thankfully to fall on the bed in my comfortable room in the Big Blue Pile and vegged out to watch a film on the satellite TV, which had two English channels, CNN and one other. The film was *Nine Months*. Hopeless drivel. One more thing Hugh Grant should be thoroughly ashamed of.

Two hours later the room maid came to collect the sixty cents I owed her for the resuscitation of my trousers. They'd had a grim time of it in the water, grass and ruinous mud of this day's frolics. Now they were restored to me washed, dried, pressed and in a state they had not been in for a very long time. My shoes would take longer to recover. After several dousings they were water-logged and squishy.

I dragged myself off the bed to eat dinner in the restaurant at the front of the hotel. Feeling that it is obligatory to try the local beer in any new country, I ordered a Beerlao, Lao's national product. The only form it came in was a large family-sized bottle. I drank half and donated the rest to the five boys who were allegedly restaurant staff. There was also one girl, who worked while the five males sat at a table beside the entrance playing dominoes and watching a television set turned up to a hideous loudness.

17 On the road again

Early next morning I tuk-tuked to the bus station planning to buy a ticket for the following day's bus to Pakse. Here I got a look at the local 'common bus'. That's pretty much what it looked like. Shabby, crowded, the only air-conditioning pouring in with the diesel fumes that wafted through its missing windows, there it sat ready to leave on that day's journey. No need to book they told me. First on, best dressed.

Just to make sure that there was not, as I'd had many reports of, a VIP bus that made this trip, I went to check with the Tourist Information Office. On my first visit there, two days ago, my friend of the shirt and tie had told me that there was a VIP bus, and even gave me its departure time – nine am.

This day he was not there, instead I found three different workers. They sat in a row in the empty office, with me possibly their only visitor for the day. The only other tourists I saw in Tha Khaek were those at the Travel Lodge. And I don't think they strayed far from its grounds. These new tourist officers confirmed the bus station's report, denying any culpability in the previous fiction I had been spun about the mythical VIP bus that left at nine am.

Abandoning the quest for VIP status, I went looking for a moneychanger. I had read that there was one near the immigration office at the river port. This area bustled with coming and going traffic – barges and other craft bringing freight and passengers between Tha Khaek and Thailand on the other side of the river. There was even a duty-free shop. It stocked only booze and cigarettes, but there was a nice waiting room, a pavilion open on three sides to the cooling breezes coming off the river.

In the street leading up to the port, long lines of trucks waited to be ferried across the river to Thailand on flat-bottomed barges. These craft had a metal ramp that a man raised or lowered by hauling on a long chain. Then the trucks roll on and a tugboat pushes the barge across the river. 'China Shipping', I read on several of the containers being off-loaded from the trucks arriving from Thailand.

I left the moneychanger flush with wads of money – one hundred dollars equals a pillow case swag of kip – and retired for an afternoon nap. In the evening I returned to the Travel Lodge, on the way there passing signs for – 'Potogopy', 'Guess House' and 'Laundry fast and clean'. Clean? I wondered what else it could be if laundered.

At the Travel Lodge my friend, Sarae, greeted me. I ordered dinner and read the last few days' happenings in the *Vientiane News*, Laos's one English newspaper. An advertisement invited me to come and see a woman dance with a ten-kilo king cobra. No thanks, I'd rather go to the dentist. I wondered about the mentality of anyone who wanted to dance with a ten-kilo snake of any persuasion, king or not. But most of all I wondered who weighed it. And how. Certainly not like I weigh my cat, holding it in my arms protesting loudly – the moggie, not me – while I stand on the scales.

I farewelled my friend Sarae and walked off intent on following her directions to the only internet access in town. I don't know if I did find it but I passed a place where I saw computer screens and they let me use one for a fee.

Unfortunately, though, as is often the case with community keyboards, it had been so ill-used that the letters had worn off the keys. I am no touch typist. Bigpond cut me off after three unsuccessful stabs at where I thought the letters of my password might be. As I have been known to ask of the taxation department, can't they tell an honest mistake when they see one?

On my long, slow walk back along the main road to my hotel I passed numerous rickety tables by the curbside at which sat lottery ticket sellers, mostly young women. I wondered if the loot would be sent on to me if I won. And what could I do with several billion kip in Australia? Once you leave the country kip is worthless. Perhaps it would make novel wallpaper. But deciding I could donate it to the poor in Laos, I bought a ticket anyway. I'm still waiting.

TV satellite dishes also stood on the footpath along with any other possible obstacle that could be dragged out there to obstruct your way. TV was everywhere. Satellite dishes hovered like great vultures or guardian angels over the humblest shanties. Mobile phone shops also abounded. The Lao have gone for these phones in a big way, possibly because the landline service is abysmal.

I passed a woman with a pole across her shoulders, a bamboo basket swinging on each end. Her small girl strutted happily along behind mum, imitating her. The tiny tot had a thin piece of bamboo across her shoulders with two plastic bags blown up with air on each end.

Getting to the bus station the next morning was no hassle. The hotel receptionist called 'yoo hoo' or the equivalent into the street and a tuk tuk popped up like magic. On the road we stopped to pick up a girl and for the first time I understood some Lao. She had said, 'To the market'. This was a Big Deal for me. So far I had mastered hello, good-bye, thank you and please. The guidebook's list of essential Lao phrases began –

Help!
Fire!
Emergency!
Police!
Go away!
I'm lost.

Reading that before entering the country would be enough to put you off coming.

Another passenger joined us. He spoke a little English and it turned out that he was going also to the bus station to catch the bus to Pakse. He told me that he lectured in IT at Pakse University, but had been visiting Tha Khaek for three days. At least that's what I think he said – our communication was a bit hit and miss. I wondered about the fact that he had no luggage, but he did have a three-day beard so it was probably right.

At the bus station I bought a ticket but as yet there was no bus. The bus did not originate here; it came from Vientiane, arriving about an hour later. I had come early to secure a seat but the bus was not crowded when we took off. Clambering over the bulky sacks of rice that filled the aisle – we picked up considerably more along the way – I headed for the back of the bus. My previous ride had taught me that this is the best option. The wide bench across the back is often not fully occupied and therefore you get more space. This position is not popular with those souls prone to travel sickness, which includes a large proportion of the local people.

My companion from the tuk tuk and two other folk joined me. The last two got off at Savannakhet and we had the back seat to ourselves after that. Time dragged. It was too bumpy to read as the old bus lurched, bumped, shook, rattled and rolled along as fast as it could, which was considerable on flat stretches. I had been told that it took two hours to reach Savannakhet, so when to my astonishment this proved to be true I held high hopes for the rest of the journey's estimate. Foolish maiden. The times I had been given were four, five, six and seven hours, depending on who was speaking. Take your pick. It actually took eight and a half.

Even with all the windows open it was incredibly hot in the bus when it was stationary. When moving, the breeze improved the situation but unfortunately we stopped a lot. I sweated up a storm but was afraid to replenish with too many fluids as there was no loo on this, the common bus. I restricted my intake until a chance at a toilet occurred and I felt it was safe to start drinking again. This came at Savannakhet, a riverside town that had been an important centre in French colonial days.

I didn't get any food, however, because I wasn't sure for how long the bus stopped. In the end I had nothing to eat all day until eight that night. Not that I didn't see an abundance of food. Every time we stopped women and children rushed to the bus windows offering skewers threaded with frogs or chicken pieces, plastic bags of sticky rice, lychees, and peanuts. Biscuits and junk food in packets also were plentiful. But no bananas, the one thing I would have bought.

We stopped frequently to pick up and drop off passengers and sacks of rice – it was harvesting time – and because the driver needed to smoke. The aisle also accommodated many sheets of timber about a third of a metre high that were stacked along the sides of the seats, requiring passengers to high step over them. It was quite an effort to get in and out of the bus but this didn't seem to bother anyone. The driver's assistant climbed over the mountain of produce in the aisle, reached a couple of vacant seats, rolled his shirt up to his armpits to combat the heat, and lay down and had a snooze.

Travelling further south the country remained lush and green and mostly flat except for an occasional mountain that rose unaccompanied near the road. Rice and corn plots, rubber trees, cows and buffalo surrounded the small villages of wooden houses. Once I saw several little brown goats taking their siesta, stretched out in positions of languid repose, looking extremely comfortable on the family's sleeping platform under the verandah of a house.

As it began to get dark a little rain fell. On the outskirts of Pakse we stopped at a big shed to offload some of the rice sacks. They looked very heavy – it took two men to lift one – and the bus crew stripped to the waist for the effort.

By the time we arrived at Pakse only a handful of passengers were left in the bus. My friend from the tuk tuk had stuck to me like glue for the entire ride and I had begun to have the uneasy feeling that he had misconstrued my friendliness – even though it was obvious that I was old enough to be his mother. The only relationship we could have had as far as I was concerned was adoption. So during the course of the ride I had invented a husband. One thing led to another and I had added three children. However, this fictional husband soon became a nuisance as I was asked to explain several times where he was and why he wasn't with me. Easy fixed. I killed him off and became a widow. That was a mistake, too. Now my New Best Friend thought I needed cheering up or worse, that I was a Merry Widow. In the space of eight and a half hours I had married, produced three children, educated them, sent them out to work, and bumped off a husband. Who says I couldn't write a novel. Or maybe I just have a talent for lying. Perhaps that's what novelists do anyway.

When my admirer started to stroke my arm I decided to pull the plug. At the bus station I declined his offer of a ride on his motorbike, food and further meetings, and with thanks, and as gracefully as possible, I retreated. He was nice and he had told me that he earned seventy dollars a week and he paid two hundred a term for his small girl's private school. So he couldn't be all that bad.

It was dark by the time the bus put me down by the side of the road in Pakse. I hailed a passing tuk tuk. They were a different breed again here, smaller, and you faced forward in a tiny shaded carriage that could accommodate two little people beside the motorbike. My bag and I just managed to squeeze in it.

I had booked a room at the Pakse Hotel and on arrival was surprised to find it six stories high and equipped with all western hotel type trimmings. Its furnishings, however, were delightfully Lao. The foyer had lots of carved wood and portly ceramic jars – some with water bubbling from them to trickle down their sides and fall into wide bowls dotted with floating frangipani flowers. The welcoming staff spoke enough English to assure me that my booking had been received, and one young man took me up a lift and along a shining dark-red tiled corridor to my room on the fifth floor.

As I cleaned my teeth I looked up to see, pictured in the bathroom mirror, the view from the window – a golden, many-peaked roof of a large temple and beyond that the brown sweep of the Mekong. Spruced up, I headed for the hotel's lovely rooftop open-air restaurant to enjoy smashing service and good food before falling into bed and sleeping soundly.

18 Pakse

In the morning I sampled a fair proportion of the Pakse's hearty buffet breakfast of Western and Asian goodies including my special favorite, dragon fruit. At the reception desk I met a genial man who told me that he was the manager. He said he was French but he looked half and half to me, French and Lao. Small and dark, he possessed the most wonderful eyes, soft, sparkling-brown and full of laughter. It gladdened my heart to look at them. I tried to ask him about the three-day boat trip on the Vat Phu I had been quoted a price for in Vientiane that travels south from Pakse, but his English was about on a par with my French so we didn't get past the basics. He handed me over to the receptionist who understood what I was on about and promised to make enquiries.

On a corner a few doors from the Pakse I found a cafe with tables open to the street and a couple of internet machines. I sat for a while at one, successfully for a change, but there were no messages – apart from the usual offers to supply me with Viagra or Russian wives – items I have yet to feel a need for. Oh well, so no one loves me, at least there was no bad news.

I learned that the cafe's owner could arrange boat or bus travel and I resolved to check this out later. But this day, I had decided, was another Recovery Day. I was tired and bone weary. I puzzled how this could be when all I had done

137

the day before was sit on a bus for eight and a half hours. Albeit hot, sweaty and uncomfortable, still I shouldn't feel as though I had spent the day digging ditches. But other travellers I met also told me that they needed a rest day after long bus trips.

Following my resolve not to do anything energetic, I went across the road and spent an hour reclining on a couch under a fan in a cool, pleasant room, stoically enduring the pain of another foot massage. Convinced that it was doing me good, I suppressed any screams and shrieks that arose in case they stopped the operator's malpractice. When the massage was over I slipped, slopped and skidded back to my room on my greased feet. I'd made the mistake of wearing the plastic scuffs I had bought in the market in Vientiane to augment my one pair of increasingly distressed shoes.

Later, venturing out to look for lunch, I stopped at a sidewalk cafe. It was far too hot for outdoor dining in the middle of the day, so I didn't find this a very agreeable meal, even though the steamed fish and vegetable dish I ordered was good. On my way back I passed a new shopping complex and went in for a look. A huge brick building with a central space like a mall, it had three floors that were reached by escalators. I decided that the local people most probably only came in here to get cool and stickybeak (like I had) and was again puzzled as to how anyone sold enough to make the rent. The goods were pretty much all the same, clothes, cheap jewellery and household plastic. This becomes boring after marching around it for a while, but I did buy a couple of pairs of knickers for a dollar each. The ones I had brought with me were disintegrating.

Back at the Pakse I retreated to my bed for a well-earned siesta and at six went to see if the desk clerk had located any information on the boat tour for me. He was off duty but, against my protestations, was called back from whence he had retired. I sat with him for ages while prices were found by phone calls to various agents but no definite arrangement could be assured, and in the face of increasing difficulties we finally called it off. I should have booked it in Vientiane when I'd had the chance. As it turned out though, I was glad I hadn't.

At the cafe on the corner I met the owner, Mr Ho, and discussed with him the options for further travel south. Deciding to eat there, I ordered a soybean vermicelli and chicken dish. The cook was Mr Ho's sister. His mother and other sister also helped, and his father, who was obviously recovering from a stroke, sat and watched over all. Later I was joined by an interesting Dutch couple and we chatted until after ten when I retired, well content with my remedial day.

Rain pounded against the window and intermittent flashes of lightning lit the room as I drifted off to sleep, and I woke to a brilliant blue morning. Commandeering a jumbo that loitered outside the hotel, I went to check out Pakse's general market. The vast Talat Dao Heung was very different from the modern shopping centre I had visited the day before. The body of this market was a huge covered area in which stalls of clothes and other merchandise were crammed shoulder-to-shoulder, while around its perimeter sellers of produce and herbal cures sat on the ground surrounded by their wares. Behind them sellers of toilet articles stacked racks of soaps and shampoos high against the outer wall, many in one-dose sachets, indicative of the depth of the pockets of a number of buyers.

Just inside the covered market, in the best, well-lit positions, the goldsellers perched behind their glass display counters. With careless unconcern they kept their money, stacks of dollars, baht and kip, in full view among the gold pieces in the cases. Finding one woman who understood some English I asked the price of some bangles, and she immediately told me that they were not real gold, only plated – the gold-plated jewellery was mixed with the solid twenty-four carat and all grades in between. An unsuspecting buyer could be easily led astray here unless the person you dealt with was this honest.

Pakse seemed even hotter than the places I had been further north. After a couple of hours sightseeing a recharge became necessary, so it was soon back to the hotel to test their downstairs coffee shop for lunch. In the lobby I was suddenly engulfed in a swarm of a hundred or so small dark people in bright-yellow polo shirts who milled about me like a flock of lost, fluffy, day-old chicks. The hotel was hosting the Beerlao convention and yellow is the colour of the beer bottle label.

The service in the coffee shop was charming, smiling but incredibly slow. It took forty minutes to get custody of a plate of any kind of food. I had chicken and cashews, which was very tasty and crunchy – the chicken was fried as hard as a board but that was how it was meant to be. In Pakse the prices didn't differ much no matter where you ate, upmarket or down. But the cost of drinks in the Pakse's rooftop restaurant leaped to three times the regular charge. It was lovely up there though and I guess you were charged for the altitude.

After siesta it was on to the evening market, which contained mostly produce – frogs, meat – and flies, lots and lots of flies, and, judging by the interest I received, is usually only frequented by locals. The Lao are too nice to be rude and stare, but it was obvious that I was as rare as a Martian here. I took a tiny tuk tuk back to my hotel, picking up a Lao woman with many bags of shopping on the way. It was rather a squeeze fitting two passengers into the tuk tuk's little seat but we managed. I noticed that no money changed hands when we dropped her off. I wondered if local people hitch free rides when they see that a dim-witted stranger, who is presumably about to be overcharged anyway, is aboard. Part of their clan system maybe. It happened often to me.

Pakse's motorbike tuk tuks either put-putted along very slowly due to the lassitude of their weary engines, or they screamed about like Formula 1 racers, whizzing around corners slantwise. If I was unlucky enough to inadvertedly choose a fast machine, being seated in front of it meant that I was offered up to the on-comers like a human sacrifice on a platter. Fortunately the wide, dusty streets were mostly devoid of traffic and what there was predominately of the two-wheeled persuasion.

Back in town, walking along the riverbank in the cool of the evening, I came across the VIP bus station. Right on the edge of the river's high bank, its waiting room had rows of seats positioned to catch the river breeze. The VIP buses, however, were all the dreaded night sleepers and off the plan as far as I was concerned. Further along the riverbank was a big, open-sided pagoda and near it a beer garden. The local people seemed to like gathering by the river. As I passed two young girls relaxing on a seat facing the water, one called to me, 'Madame would you sit with us?' I did and for half an hour they practised their English on me. They said that they hoped to improve their chance of a good job by learning English.

I walked back to Mr Ho's corner cafe and stationed myself outside at a concrete table covered with small pastel-coloured bathroom tiles and talked to Mr Ho. He told me, to my surprise, as he was around forty, that he was not married. The child he cuddled was his four-year-old nephew. All the family lived there at the cafe. Then mother appeared to take father for his nightly walk up the road. She put the child in a stroller and father, leaving his walking frame behind, used its handle to support himself and the trio set off. The sky darkened and the breeze cooled as I ate pork *laap* and the dried salted plums from Thailand Mr Ho had offered me.

By now I had discovered most of the town of Pakse although it was several days before I learned which street was the main street. It was not obvious at first as there are few shops or businesses in it. Pakse sits at a confluence of the Mekong and Se Don rivers. It was founded in 1905 as a French administrative outpost and is now the regional capital of Champasak province. The town has grown in size since a bridge across the Mekong to Thailand was built here in 2002. It has twenty temples, a large park by the river, and some rather grand, decorative French colonial buildings with extensive grounds and gardens.

There is also another Pakse Hotel, the Royal Pakse. In its pleasant sidewalk cafe the next day I met the French couple, Emile and Elise, again. They recounted the traumas of their horrific eight-hour bus ride from Savannakhet to here that was supposed to have been a mere couple of hours. Breakdowns and police holdups featured largely in this tale and they said that the heat had been exhausting. Another conversation began when Elise said that this day was the first time she had heard a Lao baby cry. I too had noticed that Lao babies don't cry. They are always held close to someone's heart.

Strolling the wide, almost deserted streets I wondered why the only car in sight was stopped at an intersection. Then I realised that way overhead, strung high across in the air, was a traffic light. Whatever for, I wondered.

Around noon I sought refuge from the heat in the Sang Aroun, a modern-looking hotel I discovered not far from the Royal Pakse. In their open, airy restaurant I sat alone and ate lunch, fish *laap* with the usual vast stack of greens and no knife to diminish them to mouth size. I did what the Lao tell me is the done thing and used my hands, the right one only of course. I wanted to try the morning glory leaves I had seen on the menu, but they weren't available. I had read that hippies were partial to morning glory seeds – and not for their nutritious benefits.

Mr Ho had arranged for me a ride on a boat down the Mekong to the town of Champasak. This was not the tourist boat I had been making enquiries about but a regular river transport craft. With supreme effort I managed to get up at five in the morning and present myself at his cafe at half-past six ready to set off for the wharf. The boat, alleged to leave at seven, finally left at half-past nine. I shall say no more!

From the cafe I was dispatched by tuk tuk to the boat landing where I was deposited by the side of the road and told to wait ten minutes. Half an hour later I asked where the boat was. By then I was sitting in the gutter under my brolly. When told 'more time yet', muttering objections, I moved somewhere more congenial. Dragging my bag up to the shade of some trees on the edge of the riverbank, I joined a woman who manned a small stall there, selling bottled water and bags of packaged biscuits. Fishing out my ever-ready book, I settled down to read. Never ever travel in Asia without some form of entertainment in your bag.

In the fullness of time a small group of passengers straggled up and we all boarded a wooden boat. This boat was like the previous ones I had travelled in up north, but it had cane chairs, rattan mats on the floor and a higher roof. We took off into a rough river swell under an overcast sky that dropped a few sprinkles of rain. The other passengers seemed to be a tour group, a Spanish couple, two Asian gentlemen and two guides who spoke their various languages.

Seen from the river, Pakse looks nothing like the river view of Luang Prabang. It is bigger with more imposing buildings. Soon we came to the confluence of the two rivers, then we were in the wide Mekong with its covering of flotsam from the recent heavy rain. There were pieces of trees – sometimes whole trunks with leafy branches – and all sorts of odds and ends that the river was rushing pell-mell down to the sea.

After a while the water became calmer. What I could see on the banks was unlike what I had seen on the riverbanks in the north. There was still a predominance of dense green vegetation, but here there were wooden houses with canoes tied near them at the river's edge. There was even a village or two, each with a bright gold and red painted pagoda rising behind it, gleaming against the luscious deep jade colour of the countryside. Near the villages grew banana trees and coconut palms.

Now and then we passed a dugout canoe being paddled along or anchored close to shore with men fishing from it, and children whooping and shrieking with laughter as they jumped into the water from trees at the river's edge. Everyone waved and called greetings to us.

After a while I began to wonder if these people with me in the boat were bound for the *Vat Phou*, the tourist boat I had been enquiring about. Then, on the opposite side of the river to Champasak, we pulled up alongside a large, unmistakably stylish boat and I was sure. I had experienced the first half-day of the expensive tour for a song. A great stack of food and supplies was offloaded onto the *Vat Phou*, along with the passengers, and I was left alone to be ferried on to Champasak.

19 Have umbrella, will travel

In the middle of the river I passed an unexpected sight. On a few planks of wood fastened across a pair of canoes, two people sat regally in cane armchairs shading themselves with a big red umbrella. What a way to travel. Although perilously perched on a flimsy contraption on a turbulent river, they looked as relaxed as if they were home on the back porch. I'd love to try this – 'Have umbrella, will travel.'

Reaching the other side of the river my boat pulled up to a small landing from where I could see nothing except a steep set of wooden steps leading upwards. My bag and I were unloaded and hauled to the top, where I discovered that I was not at Champasak but one kilometre away at the guesthouse I had called from Pakse to book a room. How the boat driver had known to bring me here eluded me – I hadn't told anyone where I intended to stay. But I know that I stick out like a sore thumb, so my whereabouts may possibly have been common knowledge.

I was delighted with the Anouxa Guesthouse – especially its absolute riverfront position. I had found the perfect peaceful spot. The guesthouse sat isolated, high above the river on the very edge of the bank and consisted of a rustically inclined row of rooms that formed an L-shape facing the water. Built mostly of wood, they had wooden shutters at the windows and a wooden verandah – the posts retaining their original tree trunk shape. Their doors opened onto small patios furnished with cane tables and chairs, a few feet from the riverbank edge.

A large deck overhung the river beside the rooms, and, cooled by the breeze off the water, served as the open-air dining area. Hammocks swung from trees on the edge of the bank and under the trees were a couple of sleeping platforms – a rattan mat covering a flat wooden base on stumpy legs. At siesta time the guesthouse family/staff distributed themselves out here. Their placid lifestyle seemed to compose mostly of eating, resting and socialising – the general the way of life in the south apparently. Just when I thought there couldn't be a more relaxed place than the Laos I had already seen in the north, along came the south to blow that theory out of the water.

My room was on the extreme end of the L part of the guesthouse, so it didn't have a patio; instead its balcony overhung the water. I could watch the river from my bed. The resident cat, a friendly little black and white moggie, came to greet me, jumping into my lap the moment I sat down to test the mattress. Bliss.

Lunch was next on the agenda. I joined a sociable French family at the wooden tables on the deck where meals were taken communally. I met the house dog, a well-mannered, sand-coloured animal that had a good dose of dingo in her.

Refuelled with food, I toddled off down the road in search of the town of Champasak. After I had completed the two-kilometre return journey and arrived back at the Anouxa, I still wasn't sure if I had seen it. Champasak is no metropolis. Strung haphazardly along the water side of the one and only road – a narrow, rutted and raddled dirt strip that runs beside the river – the town consists of widely spaced wooden houses, some good, some ramshackle, a couple of guesthouses, and the usual amount of small, vibrantly coloured temples and pavilions. But once this town was the centre of the Kingdom of Champasak and until thirty years ago the residence of Champasak's royalty.

Between the tenth and thirteenth centuries Champasak province was part of the Cambodian Angkor Empire. Later it was incorporated into the extended Lao kingdom, then at the beginning of the eighteenth century it became an independent kingdom that extended into Thailand and Cambodia. Now it is part of the Lao People's Democratic Republic. It covers the Mekong valley, the Bolaven plateau – a cool climate area where coffee, tea and spices thrive in the volcanic soil – as well as remote districts in the far east that include the Annamite mountains, home to aboriginal Mon-Khmer ethnic groups.

Walking along I rejoiced in the profusion of greenery and large shady trees that separated the buildings on the river side of the road. On the other side were rice paddies. The only shops – or more accurately, places that sold goods – were either bench stalls beside the road or the open front room of a house. By this time evening was approaching and at some of the roadside stalls women were grilling food to sell to passers-by – kebabs, sausage-like objects and bananas – on small clay or metal braziers topped with griddles.

One unprepossessing edifice, a small building set well back behind a fence and a square of grass, was suffering from the delusion that it was a post office. I would not have guessed its alleged function if a sign by the road had not informed me of it. The manner of business conducted in there must have been casual to say the least. As I moved toward it, its door was flung open and out strode a big red rooster followed by a young man wiping his bare torso with a towel.

The road eventually brought me to a small circle that I later learned was in fact the centre of the town. Here a couple of open-sided pavilions housing places to eat clung to the river's edge. I stopped at one to drink a fruit shake. Three Swedish girls sat at a nearby table. One was dressed in very short torn-off jeans and a strapless tank top – an outfit that exhibited much of her midriff and her long, long legs. The other two were only a little more covered. They were asking the staff the whereabouts of their order, placed half an hour ago. It became apparent that their victuals were not going to be delivered, so they left. I wondered if this had been a deliberate snub from the demurely dressed Lao waitresses in their long skirts and modest blouses – after the Swedish ones left the Lao ladies did a lot of giggling.

By the time I returned along the road an hour later, fat grey buffalo had been brought out to graze on the verges and ditches. They were each attached to a rope on the end of which an attendant squatted patiently, watching the placid beasts tear up and eat the lush green feed. Humans and animals alike treated the road as though they owned it, meandering all over it, never expecting traffic. I came across four elegant little brown and black goats standing in the middle of the road, trailing ropes and staring intently in one direction. They were still like that some time later when I turned around to take another look, and I wondered if their expectant stare meant that they were waiting for someone to collect them and take them home. Then an unhurried single file of corpulent white geese stalked across the road, haughtily and with great dignity, like a procession of cardinals. Suddenly, a small, pale-grey buffalo calf galloped towards me, desperately bellowing the loss of his mother. I think he expected me to help. The little silly had managed to get through the fence of the house where he and his mother were kept. Despite being amused by his comical ungainly lollop and frantic bleating, I felt sorry for him. I knew someone would rescue him eventually, but right then I was the only person around and he followed me hopefully, complaining bitterly about my indifference.

Hearing a loud clanking sound I investigated its source. It came from a cleared piece of ground between two houses where several men were playing petanque, a popular bowling game. Further on I passed boys playing volleyball with a round woven bamboo ball like those I often saw hanging in decorative bundles on shop fronts.

Back at the Anouxa, my dinner companion was another foreigner, a Canadian woman with a severely travel-worn look about her – probably caused by too much living like the natives that she seemed so proud of. Better her than me. We are not the natives! Pay the proper price expected of strangers and leave them alone. They don't necessarily want to share their already overcrowded buses and facilities with us – great big, strange-smelling foreigners who take up far more than their fair share of space.

She complained that she had come to Champasak by road because she had been told by the mis-Information Office in Pakse – which it was my good fortune to have never found open – that no boat came here. But I had seen two places besides Mr Ho's with signs outside them advertising boats.

I ordered fish soup. I knew for sure where the fish came from – a big fish tank at the rear of my room. Built of concrete under the platform that holds the rainwater tank high above, it was three metres square and had pink waterlilies floating on its surface. Earlier in the day I had watched it being drained and fresh water pumped in. Until they were big enough to be transferred to the tank, the dark silver-grey fingerlings were raised in a stoneware jar on the verandah, tended by a small girl who carefully doled out a precise measure of food to them each day.

My fish soup arrived in a washing-up sized dish in which onion, parsley, tomato and various other unidentifiable vegetables shared space with great chunks of fish that had been cleavered up – bones, fins and all. It was exceedingly good. I put some of the large bones I extracted onto the mat beside my plate and before long the small black and white cat was sitting at my elbow enjoying them. Puss had made a quiet and sneaky approach, obviously due to much practice, and I had been so engrossed in my bowl that I hadn't been aware of her presence until I heard the sound of teeth on bone. I relocated cat and bones to the floor – although I knew it was rather pointless worrying about animals on the dining table. It seemed common here. The family pets had free use of the dinner table.

That evening I rigged up my emergency lighting outfit to read in bed, one of the great pleasures of life and something I cannot do without even when travelling. Hearing the sound of a large vessel approaching on the river, I looked out and saw the *Vat Phou* tourist boat chug noisily by on what I now consider its confidence trick. The trip is advertised as being from Pakse to Pakse and it certainly is not!

I slept well despite the unbelievable hardness of the bed. It was a solid hunk of wood and I think what passed as a mattress was also wood. At breakfast I asked for fruit salad and got half a tree crop of fruit, paw paw, banana and one fruit that I didn't recognise at all. As I ate, a noisy long-tail wooden ferry clattered by; across the river's beige water I could see a village on Don Daeng Island.

The friendly guesthouse owner asked me if I wanted to go to Wat Phu. This ancient temple complex was the reason I was here so, as it seemed easier than trying to find my own way there, I agreed and he arranged for his brother's jumbo to take me there and back for a small fee.

Brother and I set off. The journey seemed longer than the supposed ten kilometres. Riding along we passed through the town. The palaces of the former royals stand, like everything else, beside the one road. I thought they looked rather run down; far from palaces, more like dilapidated French chateaux, one white, the other ochre yellow but both in need of help. Nearby Wat Nyutthitham houses the ashes of various royalties including the last king of Champasak, Chao Boun Oum, who died in 1980. Not far past the town centre there is an enormous gilded Buddha who sits with his back to the road looking out over the river, not in a temple or a pavilion, but just in a patch of shaded forest.

After the town there were rice paddies, scattered houses and another village. Most of the buildings were wooden. There were the usual amount of dogs, other animals, and kids. One tiny toddler peddled a diminutive red plastic tricycle down the middle of the pockmarked strip of road that we swerved along, dodging gaping holes.

At the entrance to the grounds of the temple complex I was relieved of a 30,000 kip entry fee, then driven to the road that leads to the temple and put out to walk. But first I had to show my ticket to a couple of uniforms on guard at a wooden table beside the entry, both of whom laboriously recorded its number and my nationality in separate books. Surely the person back at the gate could have done this. There was not exactly a mob of us clamoring to get in. In fact, I was the only visitor there at this time.

Wat Phu is an ancient Khmer religious complex, similar to but not as large as Angkor Wat, Cambodia's Angkor-era site at Siem Reap. The remains of the ancient road that connected the two can still be seen. Covering eighty-four hectares, Wat Phu sits impressively above the Mekong at the junction of the river and the mountain, Phu Pasak, up the slopes of which it stretches 1400 metres – six terraces on three levels joined by long stepped promenades flanked by statues of lions and the mythical water serpents, *naga*.

The animist spirits of Phu Phusak (locally called Phu Khuai – Mount Penis) and its freshwater spring had been worshipped from antiquity by the original tribes of the area before fifth-century Khmer Hindus built temples here. Construction continued for centuries, with additions, sub-tractions and rebuilding. In the thirteenth century it was converted to a Buddhist site but much of the original Hindu sculpture remains. At that time the temple and nearby city was the political and economic centre of the region. In 2001 Wat Phu was given World Heritage Site listing by UNESCO.

I set off toward the sacred mountain. The approach in front of me, covered with vegetation in all shades of green, was spectacular. I walked up the very long paved ceremonial promenade, lined on each side by rows of big stone lingams, stepping carefully on old, uneven cobblestones with grass growing between them. On either side, sprinkled with pink lotus flowers, was a large pond whose still waters reflected the trees and overcast sky. At the end of the promenade I reached two pavilions made of sandstone and laterite that are said to be tenth or eleventh century. Consisting of dark ancient stone, they loom either side of the approach to the mountain. Behind the southern pavilion was Nandi Hall and an ancient royal road that once ran south from it to connect with the road to Angkor Wat.

From here, broad, dark grey stone steps, interspersed with grass and edged by balustrades carved with *naga*, ascend, shaded by frangipani trees, to the top of the lofty mountain.

The entire mountain was covered with trees except for the steps, and from a distance you could not see the stone, so they looked like green stairs.

At first the climb was easy and gradual, then a set of extremely high, narrow and slippery steps – it was damp here after the previous night's rain – confronted me. Beside the commencement of the steps was a shrine. I stopped off to be given *baci*, the ritual welcome blessing, by some women attending it, then started the long haul up. The going got harder and the steps steeper, but looking back the view was sensational. On the upper level was the cave from which the spring arises and a winding path that led to Crocodile Stone – a boulder carved with a stylised crocodile, a god-like creature to the Khmer. The function of the rock is unknown but it has been suggested, though not verified, that it was a site for human sacrifice a very long time ago.

I made it to the top wheezing and puffing like an asthmatic steam engine, to discover that the hardest part was to get back down those tricky steps again. Now that I could see below me it was painfully obvious that there was a long, long way to fall should I have a mind to.

Surprisingly I made it down with no more damage than a bit of dirt acquired by the odd slip and slide, and proceeded to the exhibition hall near the entrance. This contained interesting pieces of sculpture, translations of inscriptions and facts about the site, many in English. There was also another Buddha Calling for Rain so I made an offering. When I came out it was pouring. I meant in Australia, not here, I muttered. My wires must have got crossed.

20 Island hopping

After the exertions of the temple trip I needed the rest of the afternoon off. A nap on the bed in my terrific room under the overhead fan while the river rolled by outside was in order. Later I ate dinner on the verandah and, talking to a Belgian couple and the Canadian woman, discovered that we all planned to leave the next morning for the island of Don Khong with transport the guesthouse owner had arranged.

Since leaving Luang Prabang I had been steadily heading south and Don Khong was the next step on the way. It is the largest island in the fifty-kilometre stretch of river between Champasak and the Cambodian border, known as 'Four Thousand Islands'. At this point the Mekong is fourteen kilometres across in the rainy season, the widest part of its 4180-kilometre journey from the Tibetan plateau to the South China Sea. This section of river is sprinkled with countless small islands and I planned to visit a couple. The further south one goes the quieter the life, I had heard. Mind, if I got any quieter I would be in a coma.

The next day I woke just as it was getting light and the morning was delightfully cool. Looking out I saw a woman sitting nonchalantly on the extreme edge of a small flat canoe, her sarong almost in the river. A small girl sat at the other end of the canoe, fearless of the dangerous-looking water rushing past. You could never swim against that current. Your only hope would be to float with it to the sea. The woman was pulling up fish traps, big cylinders of wire netting, and putting them back again. Now I knew what the posts I had seen sticking up out of the water near the bank were for – they were there to anchor the traps. And the gurgling sound I had been able to hear all night was the river's water pushing past them.

Because yesterday at breakfast I had been given half a tree of fruit, today I said, 'just one banana' and got half a banana tree! I shared it around.

At eight we were collected in a jumbo. Its back step was so high the young Belgians had to hoist me in. On departure the guesthouse owner presented me with a gift – a clunky wooden rice container and lid in a rattan case. Just what I needed to cart about with me. No one else got one. Perhaps he had a guilty conscience about overcharging me. Whatever. My room had been the most expensive they had; the rooms at the rear were much cheaper. Perhaps I had been meant to bargain.

The jumbo took us Ban Phaphin, a landing place on the riverbank from where we could be ferried across to Ban Muang on the other side where the road to the south ran past. The ferry consisted of a rickety wooden raft tacked onto two canoes. Passengers stood on this dubious platform clutching a flimsy bamboo rail. The four of us got on with our baggage, while another nearby 'ferry' supported a motor-bike as well as several people. Our unlikely craft travelled slowly but I enjoyed the trip. There was also a vehicular ferry, which was big but still not much more than a base of planks, and on it was a *swangwas* – a truck for transporting people – and a tuk tuk, both loaded with passengers.

On the other side of the river we sat down to wait for the minibus. When it arrived, it was already jam-packed. I squeezed in beside a large westerner and we began to chat.

When he told me that he was formerly Canadian but now lived in Adelaide, I realised that he was Larry, the man the French couple, Elise and Emile, had told me about meeting. Very shortly he discovered that I had just left Champasak. 'Oh, no,' he said. 'I was meant to get off there.' We persuaded the driver to stop, turn the bus around and take him back.

Another two hours travelling brought us to the village of Hat Xai Khun from where you can cross to the island of Don Khong. This time the ferry was a wooden boat with a roof. This luxury cost 10,000 kip, $1.25, but still some foreigners stood around arguing about the price.

I stepped from the landing at Muang Khong, the island's principal village, and straight into the guesthouse directly in front of it, the Don Khong Guesthouse. It looked nice and I wasn't hiking about if I didn't have to. The building had one upstairs floor accessed by a wonderful wooden staircase. I was taken up to inspect a room and told it was nine dollars. I moved in. The rooms went off either side of a wide, breezy corridor tiled with shiny dark-brown patterned tiles that gave the place a cool appearance. My room opened onto a pleasant balcony that went all around the outside of the building, the front part of it directly overlooking the river and the narrow road beside the boat landing. I had found another delightful spot!

Everywhere I looked was green and lovely. Many trees and sheltered seats dotted the grassy riverbank. A couple of wooden slow boats were tied at the landing. Nearby, the guesthouse owner sat dangling a fishing pole in the water. There was an even more unhurried feel here than Champasak.

On the right of the guesthouse was a green field where, looking over the low, white-painted concrete balcony edge with its bright-blue colonnades, I could see boys playing soccer. Beside the soccer field was Wat Phuang Kaew, a large temple. Two enormous *naga* serpents guarded its imposing entrance behind which an enormous gilded seated Buddha towered over the surrounding grounds against a backdrop of palms and trees.

Close by, a few metres along the riverside, was another guesthouse, Mr Pons, whose outdoor restaurant overlooked the water. As lunchtime approached I wandered down there and found the Canadian woman installed at a wooden table with a scruffy male hippie she had acquired since arrival. He already had three empty beer bottles – and big ones too – in front of him and it was barely noon. Then, Emile and Elise popped up again! We were obviously following the same trail south. I gave them a message from Larry then ordered fish *laap*. It was terrific. A large black cat materialised as soon as lunch hit the table. Fortunately there was enough to share.

I walked on from Mr Pons to see the town. There wasn't much to see, but it was great. Most of it lined the river. There were bougainvilleas, betel and other palms, flame trees, mangoes, pawpaw, frangipani, and many Indian almond trees, which, shaped like umbrellas, give wonderful shade.

Heading north up the uneven dirt road that ran beside the river from my guesthouse, I crossed a rickety wooden bridge fortified by planks that had been laid over the gaping boards by some thoughtful person in order to stop the motorbikes falling through. Along this stretch of road were two more guesthouses and the post office, closed right then for its two-or-more hour lunch break. Further on I came to a big wooden pavilion-like structure, open all around and containing rows of seats. It was so grand I couldn't work out what it was used for. But as I watched, several people arrived and, descending the wooden staircase on one side of it, climbed into a boat that shortly chugged off. It was the waiting room for boat passengers. It looked more like a dance pavilion!

There was one back street behind the road along the river and it contained the police station, a few houses and a couple of local stores. The island is quite big but there were no tuk tuks. Motorbikes seemed the only way to get about. Boats were used to go short distances up or down the coast and across to the other side of the river.

At one stage of my exploratory walk I shared the small dirt road with a white and speckledy-brown mother duck and her eleven ducklings. Although a little harassed, she was doing a good job of keeping her large brood in order. She became anxious as I got among them but she didn't attack me, although I think it was on her mind. Not like the belligerent geese I met later that I gave a wide berth to. Once you've had a nip from an angry goose you don't mess with them again.

I returned to Mr Pons for dinner and ate with my French friends and a young couple, also French. They smoked up a storm all over me. I am amazed that the French in general still smoke. They seem to have a resistance to the stop smoking campaigns. Emile told me that his mother had been warned, 'give up or die'. She chose to die. Astounding! It must affect your brain as well as your lungs.

The wine at Mr Pons was around three dollars a glass. It was a big glass and they filled it up. I had two. By accident. (That's my story and I'm sticking to it.) The first one brought to me was white when I had asked for red. So of course I had to drink it and then order another to get the red. It was very strong, rather like port, and I have grave doubts about the veracity of the label that claimed it to be a cabernet sauvignon. Consequently, trying to find my way home became a problem. I staggered up the dark, unlit road and into the wrong guesthouse. Feeling an utter fool I turned around and exited. The suspect wine didn't even have the decency to wait until the next morning to assault me. It gave me a headache before I went to bed. I took two aspirin.

At six the next morning a loud gong being struck in the temple next door jolted me awake. Then a megaphone-enhanced voice began what sounded like a communist harangue. But it may have been a monk praying. It went on ceaselessly for an hour and a half by which time I didn't care who he was, I could have throttled him.

My breakfast was brought up to the part of the verandah that overlooked the river, which was furnished with wonderful solid-wood divans, couches, chairs and armchairs. A rocker-recliner ingeniously contrived of wooden slats swung in a ponderously heavy frame, so hefty I couldn't move it. I sat down in the rocker and was catapulted backwards, flat out, with shocking rapidity. When I tried to get out again, I found I couldn't. A man-eating chair had me in its clutches! Would it gobble me up like a carnivorous plant?

After a sustaining breakfast I negotiated with Madame, the owner's wife, for transport to take me around the island on a sightseeing expedition. I set off on the back of a motorbike ridden by a nice young man who was one of the family. I was asked to pay for the bike ride before we left in order to buy petrol. A short distance down the road we stopped at the petrol station, a wooden hut two metres by three opened by hoisting a wooden flap up and supporting it on a pole. Inside the tiny hut there was just enough room for two forty-four-gallon drums of petrol. On top of each drum was a glass container graded with measurements. The fuel was pumped up into this and from there it was drained into the bike's fuel tank via a plastic tube. It cost around two dollars to fill the bike's tank.

Then off we went. To ride slowly around the entire island on the dirt road took two hours of dodging potholes, cow and buffalo pancakes, kids, dogs, geese and ducks but almost no motor traffic. There were bicycles and the odd motorbike but I saw only one truck and a *swangwa*.

The island is eighteen kilometres long and eight wide, sparsely populated, with patches of uninhabited country covered with forest. The central area is occupied by a couple of heavily wooded hills but some of the flat land between the hills and the river contains rice paddies and vegetable plots. The few houses scattered among the paddies were simple affairs of wood and rattan.

Most of the island people, largely fisher folk and farmers, live in or around two villages, Muang Khong on the eastern shore and Muang Saen on the western. The island is mostly self-sufficient, producing rice, sugar cane, coconut, vegetables and fish as well as weaving textiles.

When we came to Muang Saen, the village on the other side of the island, I dismounted to buy a coolie hat for a few cents. They hung in bunches from the top of a wooden stall by the road. I'd found it hard to keep my umbrella up in the wind of our progress. I saw other women on motor-bikes do it, but not on the open road. Bunches of lotus pods also hung, upside down like long-stemmed roses. Bright lime-green, they look unreal and more like old-fashioned showerheads than anything living. I had seen them roasted on braziers and offered as snacks.

Back at the guesthouse I sat on the balcony massaging my rear. The tiny bike had had the usual rock-hard, bum-numbing pillion seat. Directly below I could see my former escort gently swaying in a hammock strung between two trees on the extreme edge of the riverbank, also recovering.

Later I visited the post office, a small, ramshackle weed-fronted building. Three postal pixies were crowded into a tiny space behind a narrow wooden counter. It was not rush hour. I was the only customer. A stamp to Australia cost sixty cents. I sped my postcard away with misgivings, but high hopes. (It did arrive, which was more than I can say for others I have sent from far more salubrious-looking establishments in other countries.)

21 Four thousand islands

Towards evening I strolled, dodging the stones in my path, along the shaded, soft-dirt track that meandered beside the river to Wat Jom Thong, a large temple at the edge of the village. Built around the early 1800s, it is the oldest temple on the island.

Passing under the elaborate arched entrance in the white-painted wall that surrounds the temple compound, I found myself in a shadowy green gloom created by dense, spreading trees and over-hanging palms. On one side of the compound were the wooden quarters of the monks, and spread over the rest of the extensive area were a tower with a brass gong and several small stone pavilions – crumbling old buildings that added to the timeless feel of the place. As though silenced by the tranquility of the atmosphere, my feet made no sound as I crossed the sandy, grass-covered ground to where a shining golden Buddha statue sat watching the waters of the river pass by. An old monk was seated on a tree log beside the pagoda and on the grass around him several young men squatted on their haunches listening intently to his words.

Returning along the path I passed three orange-robed novice monks who smiled and said, '*Sabai di*'. I stopped to eat at the other waterside restaurant the village boasts. And drink. Or at least I tried to. Their red wine cost only a dollar a glass, which I thought cheap after my debauch of the night before, until it turned out that the price was low because they gave you only a smell of the cork in a glass the size of an eye bath. Unlike that of their competition, there was no hangover headache in this tipple.

The unattractive male foreigner I had been trying to dodge since I arrived joined me. He told me that he had been in Laos for years. He looked it. He was a classic example of a leftover hippie and a poor specimen in bad condition at that: scrawny and weedy with skin sores and a straggly beard. With not enough good food, lots of drinking and probably drugs, he had not borne the slings and arrows of life well. Drifts of empty beer bottles bobbed in his wake wherever he went.

From my riverside table I watched the most wonderful sunset. Instead of the usual flaming red and orange, the sky turned a pale bluish-mauve and pink that somehow made the river appear to be moving slower. The water, no longer looking in a rush to get to the sea, took on a molten appearance as though covered with a fabulous shimmering, gently moving silvery-pink oil. Maybe an artist could create this colour, but you could never mix it in a paint shop.

That evening my guesthouse hosted a large gathering of local people. On my way out I had seen two long tables on the ground floor being set with rows of bowls and platters, and when I returned the jolly company were well into demolishing large quantities of food and severely reducing the island's stock of beer. Lots of laughter and singing, accompanied by rhythmic clinking of forks and spoons on bottles and glasses, reached me upstairs. They seemed to be a local club of some sort, but certainly not Rotary. I've been to their meetings and they are tame affairs compared to this.

Next morning I was on the move again, heading further south down the Mekong among the Four Thousand Islands to the last island where accommodation is available – Don Khon. I had arranged to go on the boat owned by my guesthouse, which turned out to be a good idea. Mr Pon's boat, the one advised by the guidebook, was loaded to the gunwales.

Our boat set off with a complement of five – myself, two other travellers, the driver and his ally, my friend of yesterday's motorbike expedition. The pleasant one and a half-hour ride wove us leisurely among the many islands; some, almost completely submerged by the rainy season influx, had just a bit of shrub or a treetop sticking up like a periscope for the river to swirl around. There was little traffic on the water, only a couple of paddled canoes and one small wooden boat with an outboard motor. Here and there a house or a minute wood and palm village clung to the river bank, sometimes with children playing in the quiet water close by or jumping into the river from low hanging tree branches. The sound of their laughter floated across to us as they hailed our passing with enthusiastic waves.

We arrived at Don Khon, close to the Cambodian border. Similar in name to the island I had just left, Don means island. I had bypassed Don Det, which is joined to Don Khon by a bridge. It has become a traveller's hangout similar to Vang Vieng, north of Vientiane.

As I had progressed further and further south, life had become, as promised, more and more relaxed. Now I was struck with the feeling that I had landed on a place that the modern world had yet to find. Delightfully so. The spot where the boat deposited me was just a piece of riverbank. There was no landing and no sign of transport. Small sand tracks led from where I stood into palm trees that partly hid a couple of wooden houses on stilts. My bag wouldn't wheel on the sand, so, declining the kind offer of assistance from the other travellers, I enlisted a nearby motorbike rider to ferry me to the Sala Phae, a guesthouse I had read about.

It was in the main road, the 'main (only) road' being a narrow soft sand-track shaded closely by palms and trees. Its traffic was one old woman in a sarong and a dog who lay curled serenely asleep in its middle.

I was given a room at the Sala Phae, or, rather, a raft; its rooms were self-contained huts floating on platforms of logs, accessed from the bank by a rather wobbly plank walkway. Unfortunately though, the young man in charge of the keys told me that I could only stay for two nights since a French tour group was arriving then.

Meanwhile, I was supremely happy. This room was heaven on a stick for $20. There were few mod cons; there was no electricity on the island except for a generator that cranks up a bit of power briefly in the evening. The light it produced was so poor I needed a torch to find anything. But the location of this raft room – right in the water – was sublime. Walking across my room I could feel the floor moving under my feet, giving the impression that I was waterborne. And when I stood in front of my hut's open wall of glass-less windows that were almost level with the river, I had the peculiar sensation that I was moving along the river. I felt as though I had left the land and become part of river life.

Looking around I could see that this hut, constructed entirely of local materials, had been designed for coolness. The floor of wooden planks met a wall of metre-high bamboo slats followed by woven rattan sheets that stopped short of the roof, leaving an open gap for the breeze. The wonderful high-peaked roof fascinated me. It was a work of art – woven straw laid in many narrow layers like shingles, crisscrossed by bamboo poles and supported by wooden

165

rafters. Later, walking back from lunch, I watched the rain falling off a house roof like this. The entire roof was adazzle. Raindrops rolled down, bouncing from one layer to the next, a million glittering one-carat diamonds bounding from shingle to shingle until, sliding to the ends of the fronds that fringed the roof, they cascaded in a brilliant shower to the ground.

The Sala Phae boasted a restaurant, also floating on a raft on the river – a movable feast, you might say. While I ate I was entertained by the antics of a beautiful, lithe and sinuous gibbon. As big as a medium-sized dog, with short coal-black fur and white markings around his face, he lived in a large wire cage that faced the street beside the entrance to the cafe. At first I itched to set him free, but later I found that he was frequently out of his cage. Constantly active, he swung and played on a rope, turning somersaults in the air. Then he took some old pieces of cloth, draped them over his head and danced about. Spotting a shiny biscuit packet that someone had dropped beside his cage, he extended a long, skinny arm through the wire, pulled it in, and had a great time throwing it up and catching it. Then along came a man who was obviously a friend, and the gibbon sat on the floor and turned his back so that it could be scratched through the wire.

I took the remains of the enormous fruit salad I had been given for dessert and offered the gibbon watermelon and an unfamiliar green fruit that I hadn't liked. Neither did he. He touched it but passed over it. When presented with it again he took it and threw it on the ground – just in case I hadn't got the message the first time. He genteelly accepted the watermelon pieces. He knew what he liked. As he touched me with his long, soft and gentle fingers I was reminded of the lemurs in Madagascar. Then he became naughty and one of his remarkably long arms flashed out and grabbed a handful of my hair. It didn't hurt, it just gave me a scare. He obviously liked to investigate anything unusual looking. And my hair was that for sure right now, a fright wig and a strange colour to boot. Another time I saw the gibbon whip off someone's glasses. The Sala's owner told me the gibbon was very naughty but he had never bitten anyone. He seemed to be a great favourite of the local people.

Lao people appear to be fond of animals. Passing the open door of the rattan hut that was the restaurant's kitchen, I saw several half-grown chickens stalking around in there as though they owned the place, and a couple of tiny cats curled up on the floor while the cook was fondling a small, fluffy, white dog. Nice!

It started to rain while I was eating lunch, the kind of tropical downpour I usually love, but not when I had, for the first time, come out minus Pink Umbrella Mark 2. Returning hastily through the rain to my raft I skidded along the former soft-sandy path that had now metamorphosed into a slippery mud puddle. Once safely inside I sat happily on the wooden sleeping platform in front of the raft's window to watch the rain sluicing into the river. Down and down it continued and as time passed the water began to rise. Soon it was splashing over the corners of the raft. This was a tropical dream – sitting comfortably on the mighty Mekong River, feeling it moving under me, and looking out through my open window at the rain pelting down and the river water rushing past.

Across the river, on the bank of the neighbouring island, were a few widely spaced rattan and bamboo houses on stilts in front of which children were playing in the rain. I wondered whether – if this downpour continued – I might be swept away, raft and all, while I slept, waking in the morning to see Cambodia outside the window. Or maybe even the South China Sea!

I slept under a mosquito net, conscious of the sound of the river sucking and gurgling as it pressed past the raft all night and waking, opened my eyes to see it close beside me. At six a temple gong sounded and soon afterwards boats began chugging by. Off to fish or ferry people about, they put-putted past my curtain-less open windows. During the night there had been a great thunderstorm and the river had risen even higher. It was now level with the boards of the deck.

My washing facilities were housed in a corner of the raft room. The water from the tap was drawn straight from the river. It was very brown and cold and it added some interesting facets to my already bizarre hair. I had washed my shirt the night before but it was so humid here it was still damp. No problem, the heat of my body soon dried it out.

The rain obligingly stopped after breakfast so that I could explore the area of the island that passes as 'built-up'. There was little of it – a couple of bamboo and rattan shacks masquerading as stores in which staples could be bought, a couple of slowly decaying hundred-year-old French colonial villas, and a few guesthouses and traveller's restaurants along the river's edge. All the restaurants were merely open decks or pavilions and the guesthouses mostly basic affairs. But one, in the old French hospital – a mouldering once-grand stone building – was lovely. The modern hospital was also mouldering. Old and small, it was a white-painted stone house that appeared to consist of only three rooms. I read that there was no medical aid on these islands so perhaps the red cross on the wall was just decoration. Through its open door and glass-less open-shuttered windows it appeared empty. The only sign of life was a fat, placid buffalo lazily mowing the grass in its front yard.

There was no bank or post office either.

I walked the one and only dirt road to the point where

the island connected to the hippie haven, Dong Det, via a rather photogenic, prettily curved French-built bridge. Two men whose mission in life was to extract a toll from those who wish to cross the bridge manned a guard post beside it. Why two? Perhaps one man was posted there to watch the other – the traffic passing through would be minimal. I saw no one in the vicinity.

The remains of a French railway track cross the bridge to Don Det. Originally this linked Saigon and Laos. Supplies came up the Mekong, were offloaded onto a pier on Don Khon, then trundled across by the narrow gauge railway to another pier at the end of Don Det, and reloaded onto boats. This was done to bypass the thirteen kilometres of rocks and rapids nearby where the river level drops as it enters Cambodia.

The local people I passed on the road greeted me in a friendly way. The children, one dragging his toy – an empty water bottle on a string – were enchanting. Stopping at a roadside stall I bought cheese – a box of 'Happy Cow' triangles that were a poor imitation of the real article but when one is desperate they are better than nothing. I left two of the cheese triangles on the bench in my room that night and in the morning one was gone. All evidence of its existence had been removed – there were no incriminating remains to give a clue to the thief's identity and nothing else had been disturbed. I was just thankful that the rat or monkey that took it didn't have a penchant for face cream. Though it possibly tastes about the same as that imitation cheese. The Sala's manager told me that the culprit would have been a water rat. Clever little thing. Neat too.

During my investigation of the island I had found new accommodation for when the Sala Phae kicked me out. The Somphamit Guesthouse was a little further along and also right on the riverbank. The Sala's manager sent a boy to help me move after breakfast. He carried my bag to the Somphamit and I magnanimously rewarded him with a whole fifty cents at which he beamed and made me a *nop*.

Soon after I had settled in, I was off again. The Somphamit's owner had induced me to take a ride in his boat to see the nearby rapids and waterfalls. I think. I really had no idea where we were going, our mutual misunderstanding was great, but, undaunted, I climbed into his small wooden boat with the three other travellers he had enlisted in the adventure.

22 The swinging south

Our merry band of explorers – one Englishwoman, a young French couple and I – set off with Mr Gee, the Somphamit's owner, in his long, skinny, wooden and rather fragile canoe. It had a sharply pointed prow, a small noisy outboard on its rear end and a draft of about ten centimetres. Four one-buttock-wide planks across its middle served as our seats. Swiftly we skimmed over the Mekong's swirling muddy waters, passing many small and mostly uninhabited islands. Half an hour later we pulled up to the landing place of the village of Ban Nakasang, a convergence point for buses and boats bringing passengers to and from the islands.

I climbed up from the boat onto the wooden duckboards of the riverside wharf, and, sidling along its wobbly, uneven planks past the piles of goods for sale that were crammed all over it, made it to dry land. This obstacle course completed, a van awaited to take us onward. We proceeded on the most awful mud and rock track for several kilometres until we hit the road. On the way we made a detour to the bank; my companions required cash. There were no banks south of this point and they had run out of money. Mr Gee was only too keen to accommodate them. They needed the money to pay his bill.

The bank was a simple concern, a one-roomed, open-fronted office stuffed full of staff. Despite the surfeit of man-power it took over an hour, and a marathon of paperwork, to induce them to open their vault and dispense a little cash. Then the van took us south to Khon Phapheng, where for thirteen kilometres the considerable width of the Mekong becomes a churning mass of rapids and waterfalls as it thunders, wild and spectacular, down a drop in land level to rocket into Cambodia.

A fenced reserve surrounds the area from where you can view the river. At its entrance our van halted beside a hutch-like shelter harbouring two men whose job was to sell each one of us a ticket. This took a considerable time as every ticket had to be painstakingly handwritten. Moving on a few metres, we were stopped again at another hutch where the tickets had to be presented as proof that we had paid. An exercise in futility! This person could hardly have failed to see us buying our tickets a short distance away up the road.

An overhanging platform high on the river's edge served as the observation stand. Here a spectacular sight greeted us. At this point, where the Mekong pours down into Cambodia, it's as if the river knows it's going somewhere different and so dramatically changes its behavior. From its previous pace – pushing along at a fair clip but still looking reasonably safe to venture onto in a boat – it goes completely berserk! Billions of tonnes of brown, foam-topped water rages, boiling and seething, smashing and crashing over rocks and boulders as it cascades riotously downstream. The falls are not very high; it is the extent and the duration of the multiple spills that make this the largest and most awesome set of waterfalls found anywhere along the Mekong.

I stood absorbing the amazing sight with several Thai tourists. They come here by the busload. This is a site of serious spiritual significance – 'a spirit trap' – a place where the spirits of dead animals and people collect, ensnared as they are washed down the river.

Sadly, a couple of weeks after I was there, several Australians, visiting from where they had been working in Thailand, were killed by lightning during a monsoonal storm.

After viewing the amazing falls, lunch was now on the agenda, and the other travellers and I patronised an outdoor food stall, conveniently close by in a pleasant tree-shaded rural setting. I ordered fish, but, unlike the last two times I had done so, no cat appeared to share it with me. I was vaguely disappointed. After lunch it was a return from whence we came along the same route in time for a rest in my hammock before dinner.

My new accommodation, the Somphamit Guesthouse, was basic, but I loved it. Built of wood and rattan high on stilts on the extreme edge of the riverbank, it consisted of a row of three rooms and a wide verandah, under which the guesthouse boat bobbed on the water. Each room had a hammock – for swinging and river watching – tied to the balcony posts in front of it, and a tiny attached cubicle for ablutions – a toilet that emptied directly into the river, a barrel of water, a bucket under a tap to fill it, and a plastic dipper for flushing and washing. What more could you want?

I washed my hair when the generator came on and electricity for my dryer made a brief appearance. My hairdryer didn't get along with the electricity, it made protesting consumptive coughs until I took pity on it and turned it off. I think the generator was not up to speed on the required amount of volts.

My room was on the end of the row and beside the portion of riverbank that the guesthouse family, wearing sarongs for modesty, used for bathing, morning and evening. They lived in a small rattan and palm frond house at the rear of the guesthouse, apparently without in-house washing facilities. Why would you bother building a bathroom when you had the world's biggest and best right at your door?

I don't think the government-printed poster on the wall of my room that said, among other things, 'ANY DESK OR RECEPTION THAT IS IMPOLITE CAN BE REPORTED', was needed here. 'Reception' at the Somphamit consisted of the owner standing in the street, or, more correctly, the path that impersonates the street, waylaying passing trade. The clerk was his son, a callow youth, whose 'desk' was a humpy the size of a bush dunny, in which he stored some tools and his fishing gear.

The riverbank below me was also the family's fishing hole and it frequently had collections of boys dangling lines in it. I watched a little boy throwing his line in doggedly with no success until his big brother came along and began teaching him how to cast. A few feet away on the riverbank, another boy swung companionably in a hammock suspended under a tree. A little brown cat approached, climbed the steps to my verandah, sized me up, then jumped onto my lap to sway in the hammock with me.

Finally summoning enough energy to saunter two doors down the riverbank to eat, I ordered fish. After twenty minutes the smiling waiter returned and said, 'Please wait. We getting now fish.' Sometime later – time means nothing here – a young boy rode up on a bicycle with my future dinner under his arm – a large fish partly wrapped in a banana leaf, its tail still flapping. In the fullness of time I got my meal and it was delicious.

Then it was back to clocking up more Frequent Swinging Points in my hammock. The balcony of my room caught the river breeze and when it began to rain it was lovely and cool. But eventually I had to retreat inside to sleep and even though no electricity meant no fan, it wasn't too bad.

During the night I heard bangs against the verandah

poles that stood in the water – probably from passing logs – and was woken early by a posse of roosters summoning the sun beneath my room. Getting up I realised why people here go to bed and get up with the sun. Without artificial light you need daylight to find your toothbrush! I flung back the wooden shutters I had closed over the glass-less windows either side of my room and the pale golden light flooded in.

Polishing off a hearty breakfast, I hired a motorbike by the simple means of asking the rider of one I passed in the street if he would like to take me to the western end of the island, to Tat Somphamit, another place from where the Mekong's wild ride down to Cambodia can be viewed. This is somewhere the local people believe is *Li Phi*, a spirit trap. They would never enter the water here, quite rightly believing that it doesn't do to mix with the dead. Two foreigners who did so in recent times drowned.

I tied on my coolie hat, anchoring it firmly on my head with a scarf pulled tight. Excellent gear for bike travel. The ride out to Tat Somphamit on the pillion of a small motorbike is not a pursuit I would recommend for a person who had not (mis)spent part of their youth on motorbikes, or at least a horse. I needed both these accomplishments to remain in the saddle. The tiny path was stony, pitted with huge holes and expanses of mud and water, and it twisted deviously hither and thither. I bounced and bucked and lifted saddle, hanging onto the bottom of the seat for grim life. It would not have been seemly, even from the safety of my advancing years, to cling to the rider, much as I wanted to.

Leaving the few buildings of the town we rode among plots where paddy grew, occasionally passing wallowing buffalo and small naked boys playing in the mud. Then we followed patches of forest and woods until we reached the riverside again.

Dismounting, not without some relief, I walked in the bush along the edge of the river for a considerable distance, with the water tumbling, roaring and thundering boisterously along beside me. It was more of the same as the falls and rapids of yesterday but here I could get closer and commune alone with those spirits.

Following an afternoon of undiluted sloth – hammock swinging is infectious – I decided that swinging in a hammock is a pleasure pure and simple and would be a fine way to pass the next few days, occasionally getting vertical to restock my nutritional needs. It would be easy to drop out for good in Laos. I couldn't, but at least I could stay here until the imminent expiry of my visa forced me to leave.

Eventually I was induced from my lazy musings by a ruckus in the street. The gibbon was out of his cage, into mischief and having a whale of a time. I could see part of the restaurant where he lived when I looked in that direction from my balcony. Now much laughing and shrieking came from there. Curiosity aroused, I went down to see the fun.

The gibbon was swinging from a tree in the garden of the old hospital, now guesthouse, across the road from his cage. The garden was full of large trees. He zipped down one, shinned up another, and lithely and with effortless ease swooped from branch to branch, playing chasey with a group of children. One child caught him, held and cuddled him. Released, he swung back, fast as lightning, into the rafters of the open shop stall next to his home. Chased around there, he zipped out to land on the back of a passing motorbike rider. Retrieved, he then jumped back into the stall and, swinging around it from post to post, grabbed the bamboo rack that served as the shop fitting. The rack fell over and all the packets of chips and biscuits it had contained went flying. I helped restore them and set the rack upright with its feet in the saucers of water that kept the ants at bay. The little devil, seeing what good fun that had been, pulled it down again. Such is the nature of the Lao that the shop owners just laughed, and no one got cross.

Finally one of the girls from the restaurant family called a halt to playtime. Picking the gibbon up, she hugged him to her. He twined his arms around her neck lovingly and went off placidly on the back of a motorbike in her embrace. How I wish animals were always treated with such love and respect.

The next morning I tried to have a sleep-in but one rooster, more persistent than his cohorts who were performing underneath my room, perched on my balcony rail and insisted that I get up and join the human race. It had rained almost all night and the air was cool. Looking out I saw Mr Gee's son bailing the boat at the river edge.

After several days, reluctantly I had to leave this peaceful island. It was an easy exit; all I had to do was transfer myself and my bag into the boat stationed beside the steps that led up to my room. As soon as we set off it began to rain steadily and shortly I was not the only person in a canoe with an umbrella aloft. We travelled along the river to the landing place at Ban Nakasang, the village from where we had taken off on our trip to the waterfall. Mr Gee dragged the wheels of my bag through the mud of the road to a small minibus that would take me back to Pakse.

Then I waited. The driver was hoping to fill the small, already crowded bus further. An hour later we took off. From the window all I saw along the road to Pakse was grey and drizzly countryside.

23 A fond farewell

It was still raining slightly when I arrived at the minibus terminus in Pakse. There I discovered that I had landed just around the corner from the Pakse Hotel, my intended destination. The minibus office displayed a sign outside that claimed it was able to arrange train tickets through Thailand to Bangkok. Inside a man was sleeping soundly on a wooden couch but my noisy scratching about the place failed to wake him, so I desisted.

The Pakse receptionist remembered me and offered me my old room. All the long ride here I had been dreaming of the Pakse's luxury – soft beds, nice bathroom and bright lights. I wallowed until teatime. By then it had stopped raining, and, thinking it safe to go just a short distance to the Royal Pakse for dinner, I left without my brolly. Murphy had other ideas. As soon as I sat down in the pavement cafe it began to pour. And pour. I sat watching the torrents sluice down, thinking it would stop but it got heavier and heavier until by the time I was ready to leave there was a deluge. Out in the street bike and motorbike riders splashed past holding umbrellas and the tuk-tuk drivers had encased themselves and their passengers in cocoons of plastic. The kind waiter searched for an umbrella to lend me, but couldn't find one. So I streaked – well, ambled fast – across the road to an internet cafe, intending to occupy myself until the rain, hopefully, stopped. All six machines were in use so I sat down at the other end of the room with one of the staff, a young girl, and we chortled away at the cartoon hour. By the time the cartoons were over the rain had stopped and I could slosh back through the sodden streets to the Pakse.

In the morning it was still raining hard. I took a jumbo to the market, chickening out on getting wet and blown about in a tuk tuk. And then it really rained. Oh boy, how it rained. Drenching torrents poured down non-stop. You start to think after a while that it can't keep going, but it does. It was dark in the covered market and the din on the tin roof was deafening, even drowning out the racket of the music stalls.

Returning, I walked around the town and realised that, as it was Sunday, many places were shut. The bus station on the river was open but the girl on duty there told me that they don't sell tickets for the international bus to Thailand. This bus takes you across the border to where you can catch the train to Bangkok. I bought my ticket instead from Mr Ho, the owner of the cafe near the Pakse, where his old dad and his sisters greeted me warmly.

After lunch I went for another massage. This time I opted for a Lao full-body massage for 35,000 kip ($4.50). I was given a pajama suit like a karate outfit to put on and the small woman masseuse and I got down on the floor. This little woman then proceeded to pull my legs and arms about, twisting them into corkscrew shapes. I was bashed and pummeled mercilessly. Even my head was knocked about. Resistance was useless even though this tiny scrap of a person who was either sitting or standing on me was half my size.

Released, I returned to my room to prepare to exit Laos.

At eight in the morning I was in Mr Ho's cafe waiting to be transported to the bus. Surprisingly, a proper car was used to ferry me there, not the expected tuk tuk. And it was Mr Ho who drove me. And got me sorted out when we arrived. You cannot get on the bus without completing passport formalities. Fair enough. I didn't want any more difficulties with Thai border officials. The bus was full of Lao and Thai people, and someone was already ensconced in the seat my ticket entitled me to. I found another and we left.

It took one and a half hours to reach the border, stopping a few times to collect people along the way. At the border we trooped off the bus to walk through the control. I was very careful not to bypass anything remotely resembling a checkpoint. Once again I was the only westerner. I got quite twitchy when an official with the same uniform as the one that I had all the bad memories of scrutinised me. Even before I became an illegal immigrant at the last Thai crossing I had always felt guilty at places like this. Only in Australia am I totally at ease.

A long walk across no man's land took me to where the bus was waiting on the Thai side. The day was overcast and there had been rain here too. I introduced more mud to the collection I had already acquired on my shoes and bag, adding to their rapidly increasing dilapidation.

Another two hours in the bus and we were in Ubon Ratchathani. I found a Thai three-wheeled tuk tuk to take me to the train. The driver rode straddling the bike front and I sat high in a little seat behind him. It was a long way on a big divided four-lane highway. Perched on this contraption that sounded like a lawn mower on steroids, we zoomed, rattling fit to bust, along the outer lane, passing streams of modern, up-market vehicles. At the station I had three hours to wait for the Bangkok train. I bought a ticket, had a meal of something unidentifiable from a look-and-point line-up of dishes on a stall and read. It wasn't an unpleasant wait. Finally I took up a position on the platform and talked to a Thai traveller who helped me work out which platform my train would pull in to. It arrived puffing and snorting, three carriages long.

The train attendants had great uniforms. The hostesses wore smart, tailored, mid-thigh beige minis with a fitted top and an artfully draped matching scarf. Very superior beings, they ignored my questions about turning up the heat, possibly because they had no English. Then the ticket collector came along. Resplendently decked out in a fabulous get up topped by a much-decorated hat, he looked like a four-star general at the very least. Even his uniform intimidated me. I was the only westerner in the carriage and the rest of the passengers watched me with interest. I hoped it was just because they were all admiring my nose.

Late that night the train pulled in to the Bangkok railway station and I sped to a nearby hotel to wait for the next day's flight home.

24 But wait, there's more!

I returned to Laos the following winter. It's not always wise to go back to a fondly remembered place. Time changes places but it also changes the person seeing them. However, I was sure that Laos would still be delightful and I had missed some parts of the country on my previous visit.

So now I was back obeying signs that told me to leave my shoes and any artillery I was carrying at guesthouse doors, and risking the consequences of washing my shirt in bathroom sinks.

Once again I reached the Lao border via an overnight train across Thailand from Bangkok. But now I went over the Friendship Bridge on the newly completed train line. So far it only continues for a couple of kilometres towards Vientiane but plans exist to extend it eventually all the way to China.

This time crossing the border and passing through Immigration was a breeze – not the ordeal it had been before. I was on my best behaviour, a model tourist now.

I stayed in Vientiane for a few days enjoying its tranquil way of life, happy to be warm again after Australia's winter. My room in the Intercity Hotel looked down onto the Mekong riverfront. Once an attractive outlook, now it was a scene of complete desolation. A massive redevelopment of the riverfront was taking place – not very thrilling unless you happen to be into big trucks. I was told that they were making a park for the Vientiane people. Sounds like propaganda, I thought. It's most likely aimed at the tourist buck.

The Mekong water level was noticeably low. There had not been much of a rainy season yet. Cattle grazed on a sandbank in the middle of the river on which grass and trees grew. Men waded and fished near the shore. But that evening it rained heavily so it looked hopeful that the monsoon was on its way.

The Lao had not changed. You still had to watch them converting kips, baht and dollars or the change they gave you when you bought something. Not that they would cheat you, but themselves! The first day a second-hand bookseller told me not to buy the guidebook I was looking at. He said, 'You don't want. Is fake!' And my computer case that I left behind in the hotel lobby was given sanctuary at the desk until I returned for it.

I bought a bus ticket to Vang Vieng. Surrounded by spectacularly beautiful karst peaks on the Nam Song River and notorious for riotous living, it is four hours north of Vientiane. I had given it a miss when I was here last but now I wanted to see its legendary loveliness (my story).

I sat alone in the bus labelled VIP for an hour until all hope of further custom was extinguished and I was shunted into another bus. Hot, darkened by drawn blinds and packed with foreigners sprawled sleeping across seats and aisles, this weary-looking bus had travelled overnight from Chiang Mai in Thailand. Several of the men got off to visit the toilet bare-chested and clutching beer bottles. They were on the Indochina party trail. I learned that after seven days in Vang Vieng most of them would fly out to bestow their dubious presence on Vietnam. They had no apparent interest in Laos. On the way to Vang Vieng we went through the stunning scenery blind. This lot were not interested enough to even lift the window shades and have a look. Fortunately I had seen it before.

The bus terminated at a guesthouse in the centre of Vang Vieng whose owner kindly phoned the Vang Vieng Lodge where I intended to stay. In the forty minutes that I waited to be collected, I was appalled at what I saw. I am now a candidate for the TV show Grumpy Old Women. I felt like giving most of the girls who passed a good slap. What were they thinking? Obviously nothing. Barefoot and in bikinis! In the street! Large white bosoms falling out of skimpy bras. The boys with them attached to bottles more often than not. One man went past saying he was going to sleep alone that night. By the look of him I'd have said that this wouldn't have been too hard to achieve.

Apart from the Frenchman who had advised me before not to come here, later I met a younger one who surprised me by saying how shocked he had been at the bikinis. Not something I'd have expected from a Frenchman – they are generally thought to be not averse to the sight of a bit of flesh.

In the fullness of time a vehicle arrived driven by a smiling Lao man who said his name was Mr Bess, the lodge manager. I think. His vehicle was a daggy old utility air-conditioned via glassless windows. The Vang Vieng Lodge was, depending on whom you care to believe, fifteen, seven, ten, or twelve kilometres out of town (the internet, the guide book, the guesthouse owner in Vang Vieng and me) – but the lodge manager said that it was actually nine.

We turned off the road and climbed a steep, rutted mud track to where several detached bungalows on wooden stilts clung in an ascending single file to the edge of the high riverbank. Built of the same materials as the nearby village houses, they had wooden frames, bamboo and rattan walls, glassless windows that I was glad to see were screened – this

184

looked like paradise for bugs – and four-poster beds voluminously draped with mosquito nets.

Each bungalow was secluded from the others by trees and flowering shrubs and faced a sheer drop down masses of greenery to the caramel-coloured, fast-flowing Nam Song. On the opposite side of the river blue-green foliage-covered karsts rose, sharply-pointed peak after peak.

In the evening I walked to the bottom of the hill where meals were served in an open-sided shelter covered by a thatched roof that was held up by tree trunks – one a large tree still in full leaf and flower. Nearby on the riverbank the people from the village were performing their evening ablutions – men, women and children – bodies, hair, teeth, clothes. Now and then a canoe came across from the opposite side of the river, moving sideways against the rushing rapids and rips of the water. Through the screen of trees that lined the river's edge I glimpsed rice paddies . The village plots and vegetable gardens were over there and some villagers were still returning from work.

It rained that night. It hadn't rained for a few days but once it started, oh boy, did it rain! Tremendous thunderclaps right overhead woke me at one am and through the gaps in the walls I saw brilliant lightning flashes. The deluge kept up for several hours and I began to think about the landslides which are prevalent in Laos. I had visions of the bungalow, complete with my slumbering body, tumbling down, down into the river.

In the morning I discovered that my fears had not been altogether groundless. A fair-sized tree lay fallen, water-logged roots pointing heavenwards, beside the small stream that now pelted down between the bungalows to join the river. Following the incredible night of rain it was blissfully cool and across the river thick white scarves of mist twined about the mountains.

I may not have been entranced by Vang Vieng town but I liked the time I spent at the Lodge, close to village life. I especially liked the animals that roamed at will, free-ranging where they pleased. I wondered if they were communal or whether their owners knew them well enough to recognise them. I heard prowling, grunts and bellows under my bungalow and calling cards were left! At my door two large, sloppy cowpats awaited the unwary foot. (Surveying the messages the geckos had sent down from the roof I remembered an old farm joke:

'A little birdie flying high,
dropped a message from the sky,
as the farmer wiped it from his eye
he said, thank God the cows don't fly.')

The cows here were a light tan colour and small and sweet-faced. Even the bulls had lovely, big soft doe eyes and looked so gentle I needed a quick check of their personals to be sure of their gender. The nanny goats were a darker toffee brown and they stepped daintily and sure-footedly about on the steep slopes, while a big black billy with fiercely curved horns strode past my verandah along the narrow dirt path on the cliff edge. There were numerous pigs. One fat, brownish-black sow lumbered around, rooting in the undergrowth accompanied by her five delicately tripping piglets. The babies were brown with pale pinkish legs and they looked at me with bright little piggy eyes as I walked down to breakfast. The sow gave a loud warning grunt as I approached and stood eyeing me balefully until her brood obeyed her summons and returned to her side. I stepped wide around them. Motherhood in sow form is a force to be reckoned with.

I was the only guest at the lodge so I had the place to

myself. Dinner the night before had been good for a couple of dollars and breakfast was even better – free. A platoon of chooks came to beg around the table, several scrawny black pullets and a big red and black rooster who was hen-pecked by the large grey hen who was the flock boss. As soon as I got up to leave they all jumped up onto the table and began clearing up the crumbs.

Then it was time to venture down to Vang Vieng for another look, hoping that perhaps my first impression had been wrong and I could discover something that was still nice about it. If there was I did not find it. There were lovely places like the Lodge in the surrounding countryside, but in exploiting the beauty and peace of this village all its charm had been obliterated. It did not feel in any way Lao to me. New guesthouses for foreigners were being built everywhere I looked. I walked along its streets passing one sign after another advertising pizza, tours, kayaking, trek-king and tubing – floating down the river on a large inner tube. I liked the sound of that. But drinking and drugs are common activities and it is a mistake to mix these with river adventure. Several people have died trying. One shop I passed had earplugs prominently displayed, an indication of what the nights were like. And where I sat for a rest a girl wailed that overnight someone had pinched her forty-dollar thongs. Not a Lao I bet. 'Take a walk around town looking at all the foreigners' feet,' I said. Maybe it was still possible to find a pleasant outlook onto the river but the noise from the partying must have still permeated it. It's hard to say whether I would have liked this party town when I was younger. The hippies of the 70s who began the love affair with Asia were more interested in melting into local life than changing it.

By the time I had strolled the streets and the riverfront and checked out the market, I'd had enough. I flagged down a tuk tuk and returned for dinner at the Lodge. I had a marvellous noodle soup that contained an assortment of additives, including some mysterious objects that looked like mushrooms – not the 'Happy' sort I hoped. 'Happy' preceding an item on a Vang Vieng menu is not the kind of happy you get at McDonald's. This 'Happy' can get you a seriously altered state of mind which may or may not include happiness. It means it can contain magic mushrooms, marihuana, speed or opium.

The next day I was off again heading in a north-easterly direction to Phonsavan, the town nearest the Plain of Jars that I had also missed on my previous visit. Mr Bess's wife (Mrs Bess, I presumed), obtained a bus ticket for me and I paid for it and my room account with US dollars. They boomeranged! The bank said they didn't like the look of my money – the notes were not pristine enough. Filthy lucre? Mrs Bess let me work out the amount I owed in baht. Oh the little innocent. No one who knows me would trust my maths. Then I had to remind her about my laundry bill. I had done the right thing for once and sent my shirt off to be washed. The price for laundering is ludicrously cheap in Laos but when I saw my shirt I remembered why I don't usually take advantage of this bargain. It returned bearing the bruises and scars it had acquired while being beaten mercilessly with a stick on a rock in the river.

The driver of the bus to Phonsavan had been told to collect me beside the road. Two tiny motos ridden by the two guesthouse ladies delivered me and my bag down there, waited with me under the shade of the wayside stop, put me aboard and waved me off. The bus was an eight-seater van and only ten people were aboard, so the six hour trip was OK. We stopped twice for refreshments and each time I managed to find a decent loo. The second I was guided to by a monk who approached me to practice his English. He told me that he and the busload of monks with him were going to Phonsavan for a big religious festival at the local temple. Buddhist Lent started soon.

I was now in Xieng Khuang province. Between 1964 and 1973, during the American War, this was one of the most heavily bombed places in Laos, which in turn was the most heavily bombed country per head of population ever. And it was neutral! The original provincial capital, Xieng Khuang, and all the other towns of the province had been almost totally destroyed. In 1975, after the end of the war, the new communist government made Phonsavan the capital. Bomb craters abound throughout the province and UXO – unexploded ordinance – is everywhere, still causing death and injury.

In Phonsavan the bus was met by a couple of lads offering accommodation. I went with one to a place I had read was acceptable. The Maly Hotel is a distance from the main street but the outlook from the hotel's upstairs rooms compensated for that. From an entire wall of window I looked out on a tranquil vista – lotus leaves floating on a pond, followed by a series of vivid green rice terraces that flowed to a line of blue mountains in the distance. Here and there a wooden and thatch farmer's house and mango, banana and paw paw trees interspersed the paddy fields.

But the Maly's overindulgence in threatening signs was a worry. Never before had I seen a list on a hotel wall detailing what you would be forced to pay if you damaged or purloined the room equipage – one hundred US dollars for a tacky Chinese bedspread for a start. And I was told at every corner that I left valuables in my room at my peril. As for the warnings about misuse of the hot water system, all they did was confuse me! I couldn't understand what passed over what 'technicality to naked the heat'. I was left with no idea how to do the right thing by the pesky hot water system. All the sign did was make me terrified of it and it was scary enough to begin with – knobs, levers, screws, but not a tap in the usual sense in sight. But I did like the laundry list that offered to –

Wash you under lips
And shocks
And your sout engorge
[Underwear – slips, socks and bras, (Sout engorge!).]

Again I was alone in this hotel except for a posse of pilgrims who got up noisily to go and be holy at the temple at five am. That got me up and washed early, which was a good thing because the electricity went off at six, and the water, not to be outdone, followed shortly after. They both stayed off all day. Murphy was here and he had enlisted aid from all his cronies. Sunday therefore become an enforced day of rest.

After breakfast I took what they told me was a short stroll to the main street – it was more like two and a half kilometres. Phonsavan is not a very exciting place. Traffic was sparse. I wandered around the two long, dusty streets that constitute the central part of the town but much of it was shut because there was no power. It made a brief appearance for a few minutes at seven pm, then went off again. A fire had broken out in the petrol station a short distance up the road from the Maly. The power returning forcefully had been too much of a shock to their electrical system. It had caused an explosion, then a fire that burned the garage and several houses.

Returning in the dark after eating at a place decorated by bomb shells and called Craters, the tuk tuk I was in was halted at a road block diverting traffic away from the fire.

We then came to the hotel by a roundabout route and at first I didn't recognise the place in the pitch black night. I wondered why the driver was waiting on the other side of the road then I realised that he was making sure I was all right. The power finally returned around half past eight but no water. That was being used by the firefighters I guessed. I didn't begrudge it to them – we were not very far away from that fire. A dry clean before bed was the order of the day.

The next day I found the big Chinese market and bought a cushion for future bus rides. Insurance against bum-numbing seats, seventy cents got me a fine bottom-bolster with an elaborate silk-frilled cover. I went in to the UXO information centre where I cried and gave them all the kip in my purse. Even twenty dollars clears a patch of land. After thirty-five years, UXO still kills and maims people and keeps them poor because they are afraid to work their fields. I wonder why the people who dropped the bombs have not been asked to come and remove them. Like the sign at the Darwin Croc Farm says – Persons who throw objects into the pool with the crocodiles will be required to retrieve them.

Everywhere I looked throughout Phonsavan I saw old shells and bomb casings that had been used for decoration or as functional items – plant pots, barbecues, fence posts. Vegetables grew in one as big as a canoe at the Maly, while an entire wall of the dining room was covered with an arsenal of collected weaponry – big and small guns, AK-47s.

Despite the Maly's intimidating signs, Madame, the proprietor, was very kind. She told me that she had run the hotel alone since her husband died suddenly ten months ago. In the morning she found me a tour to Thong Hai Hin, the Plain of Jars, which is a few kilometres from Phonsavan. I squeezed into a minibus packed with a bunch of Brits and

Germans as well as a pair of Lao students who had come to practice their English. I didn't see the boy open his mouth. He was, rightly so, petrified of us.

The Plain of Jars, which is currently awaiting World Heritage listing, was far more impressive in real life than the photos I had seen of it. This megalithic landscape is situated on the Xieng Khuang plateau and is actually not one plain but many. On these sites clusters of various-sized jars, each carved from a single solid stone boulder – granite or a conglomerate like sandstone – sit on otherwise empty slopes and fields. Dated to the Iron Age, from 500 BCE to 500 CE, they are thought to have been associated with prehistoric burial practices. When I saw how big they really were – I could easily have stood upright in one of the largest – I wondered not only how they were made but how they were moved. The main site has several hundred jars, most weighing between six hundred kilograms and one tonne, but some weigh as much as six tonnes.

We entered the area after strict warnings about staying on marked paths. Bomb craters dot the landscape and there are many UXOs. This locality was heavily bombed in daily attacks by American planes – the Pathet Lao and the North Vietnamese had anti-aircraft guns positioned here as well as an underground arsenal. Standing in the quiet of the peaceful hilltop among these mysterious lumps of stone it was hard to imagine the desecration that had occurred. Two thousand of the jars were destroyed, all the villages and towns were obliterated and the entire population had to flee or take refuge in caves.

My tour this day turned into a seven hour marathon. After the Plains we were taken to a Hmong village to view the inhabitants. This somehow made me uncomfortable and apart from saying hello to their two charming charcoal-coloured pigs I wandered away. Then it was on to a whisky village. In a shed like a stable, vats of it sat on the dirt floor. I swear I never want to see another whisky village. At this one we were made to taste the evil-looking brew and the communal cup went around four times. But I was cheered to discover from a German chemist, fortuitously in the group, that rice whisky cannot send you mad, blind or kill you as other home brews can. Now all I had to worry about was whether other sharers of the cup had a communicable nasty.

We had a quick look at the remains of the former capital, Xiang Khuang, which is now regenerating, and another visit to a Hmong hill tribe village where I had a rest in the van.

25 The Caves of the
Pathet Lao

After three days in Phonsavan I decided to continue further
north-east to Xam Neua, the capital of Hua Phan, one of
Lao's two most remote mountain provinces. From Xam
Neua it is eighty-nine kilometres to the Vietnamese border
and thirty to the caves at Vieng Xai, which were the former
headquarters of the Pathet Lao. Until very recently this
sacred communist site was off-limits to foreigners, but now
that I could go it seemed a good idea.

Xam Neua was said to be ten hours away by the only road
that goes that way, so very early in the morning Madame
established me in a tuk tuk and told the driver to deliver
me to the bus station and deposit me in the vicinity of
the Xam Neua bus. This he did, but first we took a young
woman to the market with a couple of big plastic tubs of
rice covered by banana leaves. The driver carried them in
for her and took on another passenger before finally I was
at the station.

I was glad to see that the Xam Neua vehicle was a
minibus – hopefully it would be safer on narrow roads
with hairpin bends. We started off with eight passengers
but trawled the district collecting more until we were at
capacity with the aisle crammed as well. An hour out of
Phonsavan we picked up two Dutch cyclists. They were
thrown up on top (the bicycles not the people). They
were middle-aged (the people not the bicycles) and should

have had more sense than to be trying to pedal up these precipitous mountains. At this point I asked the driver 'hong nam?' – toilet – and he held up two fingers, which I hoped meant two minutes. It actually meant two kilometres, but was only a patch of grass by the side of the road. Most of the passengers were male. Need I say more? It wasn't only visions of lurking UXOs, but the absence of large trees to hide behind that had a lot to do with my reluctance to join them.

A very long four hours later we stopped for a break at Nam Noen, a junction where the main road branches off to the north-west and the wild ride to the far north-east, where the Vietnamese border begins. The scenery was incredible and the air became cooler and cooler as we climbed ever higher. This, the only road through the mountains, was a narrow, winding path that until very recently was a dirt track. Before it was paved it must have been terrifying. Rising to dizzying heights on green mountain slopes, the road corkscrewed around and around. We were so high that sometimes the valleys I looked down into were filled with drifting cloud. Grinding painfully up, rocketing down, it occurred to me to wonder why I was there. I had not intended to come out onto 'roads less travelled'. But someone had written 'it's off the beaten track' and 'only a few hardened or determined travellers venture through this way', statements guaranteed to get my attention. So there I was doing what I keep vowing never to do again – travelling a road that came a close second in the Scary Stakes to the Death Road of Bolivia that I thought had cured me of mountain roads forever.

But these mountains were more beautiful. The sheer height of their vertical forest-covered slopes unmarked by any sign of habitation was breathtaking. At long intervals there would be a wood and thatch house or two clinging to the edge of the road, a precipice behind. You wouldn't want to sleepwalk out the back door. The villages of Xam Neua's hill tribes were few and far between.

I blessed that seventy cent cushion on this long, rough ride. It was the best seventy cents I have ever spent. Then a tyre blew! – fortunately when we were on the inner side and not the flying-off-into-space side of the mountain. Murphy must have been on his day off. Amazingly it happened right beside a spot where a spring trickled out of the mountain to fall into a rock pool, creating a fountain at which travellers could drink, splash their faces and soak their feet. It looked much used, probably by the hill tribe people who walk this way. We passed very little traffic of any sort, a couple of duk duk tractor-carts and now and then a person pulling or pushing a handcart. Sitting by the roadside while the tyre was changed, I watched three cows treading the slope above like mountain goats, their bells ringing on the clear air.

Following the revolution, due to Hua Phan province's remoteness, it became the site of re-education camps where thousands of opposition supporters were imprisoned or used as forced labour. Many died, food was scarce and there was no medical aid. The government has never admitted that these camps existed and although most were supposed to have been closed in 1989 it is believed that one or two still remain. It was in a camp close to Xam Neua that the Lao royal family, the king, queen and crown prince, all perished and were buried in unmarked graves. Foreigners are discouraged from visiting this area and treated with suspicion if they venture near. It is not a good idea to ask.

Ten hours and a bit hours from Phonsavan we made it to Xam Neua. I liked the town the moment I saw it. Perhaps because it was such a welcome sight after the ride there. A pretty, quiet little settlement in a small picturesque valley at a height of twelve hundred metres, Xam Neua is surrounded by bright green rice paddy and enclosed by sheltering green-blue mountains. Its few streets lie either side of the Nam Xam River and are connected by two big white painted bridges.

I moved into the most expensive room in the best guest-house in town. It cost ten dollars. Then I went out in the dark to seek food. It was seven pm and almost nothing remained open except a restaurant close to the guesthouse. And by eight the entire town had closed for business.

My room was comfortable if strangely shaped – it followed the corner curve of a building beside the river. In the morning roosters woke me and I looked out into the big trees that bordered the river. The encircling mountains were now obscured by mist as I watched a woman wade into the river to wash clothes on some large stones that protruded from the water.

At the tourist Lack of Information Department I asked directions to a guesthouse that allegedly arranged trips out to the caves of the Pathet Lao at Vieng Say. I was told 'straight on, you can't miss it'. To Murphy's Law – Whatever can go wrong will go wrong – should be added – If they tell you can't miss it, you will!

The tourist office staff were the only people I found in Xam Neua who had any English and theirs ranged from limited to nil. And even though I had progressed to being able to say 'toilet' in Lao, I was doing a lot worse than they were.

Giving up on the mythical guesthouse I took the only way I could find to get to Vieng Say, a *swangwa*. Thirty kilometres of more stunning scenery later, in a narrow valley protected by steep limestone cliffs, I found the office where I had to register to visit the caves and was assigned a good-looking young man as my guide/guard.

My escort and I set off and I learned that in 1964 the

leaders of the Pathet Lao sought sanctuary in this deep warren of caves that the cliffs made impregnable to air or land attack. From here they carried on their resistance until 1975 when the war ended and they assumed control of Laos. There are around four hundred caves in the vicinity and in them twenty-three thousand local people also sought shelter during that time in order to survive the bombing that destroyed all life outside. They must have been desperate days. The caves may have been safe and some of them are huge but I found them damp, dark and depressing places. However, all aspects of life continued in them – they even had a hospital and sports facility.

I spent a few more days walking about Xam Neua's tranquil streets and visited the two war memorials, one for Lao soldiers and one for Vietnamese. Immediately behind the street that runs along the river's edge, bright green rice and vegetable plots flourished and animals wandered. I met only a couple of foreigners and even though the local people looked at me with curious eyes they still smiled and greeted me with 'Sabai di'. Once a tiny toddler, one hand clutching a battered doll and the other stuck firmly in her face, stared saucer-eyed at me, fascinated. Then she pulled out her thumb with a pop and uttered one word, 'falang', which means foreigner. Although I suspect it also means foreign devil. And weirdo. Passing the Department of Industry I thought that the man sleeping soundly across their doorway said it all about this laid-back place.

With the exception of going north to the Vietnamese border, the only way out of Xam Neua was to retrace the road back to Nam Noen and either continue south to Phonsavan or head up the north-east road into more remote areas. I wanted to travel by boat via the Nam Ou River down to Luang Prabang. By asking a couple of foreigners going through on the overland route to Vietnam what the river was like, I learned that I would have to go all the way north, another twelve hours of mountain road by bus to Nong Khiaw before the river level would be high enough for boat travel.

This time the bus was an eight-seater people mover into which were squashed twelve Lao men with me inserted in the middle like the filling in a Lao sandwich. At least I had no worries about suffering any damage if we fell over the edge. I was airbagged all round. The ride was hot, sweaty, and so much for the fabled beauty of this part of the country. I saw nothing except the bodies and heads of the people surrounding me. The road passed through a National Protected Area where there are tigers, clouded leopards and other wildlife, but the only animal life I saw was my Lao companions.

Around twelve hours later I was put down in Nong Khiaw and the bus went on south to Luang Prabang, another six or seven hours away. No transport of any kind existed in Nhong Khiaw except that which was passing through, and the Riverside Lodge that I wanted was a long walk away on the other side of the river. A kind girl at the eating place the bus had left me beside phoned the Lodge. They had no rooms that day. Undaunted I moved into a guesthouse that was fortuitously next to where I was. It consisted of several simple bamboo and rattan bungalows that overhung the riverbank that, although rather wobbly, were ridiculously cheap for such a terrific setting. From a shaky verandah surrounded by tall trees, I looked down on a lovely garden along the river's edge – trees, palms, creepers and bushes in many shades of green sprinkled with white, yellow and red flowers.

Later I strolled across the long impressive bridge over the Nam Ou River that divides the sleepy village of Nong Khiaw, pausing now and then to look down on the river craft passing up and down. A short way from the beginning of the bridge I could see a flight of steps leading from the top of the bank down to the boat landing where several blue riverboats were tied up.

On the other side of the river there were a couple of guesthouses, but Nong Khiaw is a small village and few travellers stop here. The Riverside Lodge, the place that had rejected me, was reached via an almost perpendicular dirt track. It had an even more superb setting than the guesthouse I had moved into and its fittings were flasher. I booked a room for the next day and the gorgeous young manager promised to send some transport to collect my bag and me in the morning.

Sometime during the night it rained heavily. Standing on my balcony in the early morning, I gazed out at a cool, new-washed world. Tendrils of pale white cloud drifted along the mountains. It looked primeval. I felt as though I was waiting for the world to begin. Like this was the first morning on earth in the Garden of Eden.

Then the rain began again, increasing until the mountains were obliterated. The downpour continued hour after hour, getting heavier, as I waited for the promised transport to the Riverside. And waited. I phoned several times and each time I was told it was coming. Finally it arrived – in the shape of two small Lao girls, smiling under umbrellas. They were the transport across the wide bridge and up the steep mud track under umbrellas in this deluge? No way. The bag would be soaked. And me. And the sweet girls. I waited some more but the rain did not give up, I did! I moved back into my room again.

The next day I was successfully moved across to the Riverside. This time by a giggling trio – the two wee girls and an even wee-er boy pushing a wooden handcart with much hilarity. My latest bungalow was set high on the extreme edge of the river and faced a series of pointy-peaked karst mountains that the river cut through. They were covered with green jungle, splashed now and then with bare patches of limestone streaked with yellow and white. From across the water, which was now the same tan colour as the cows, fast-flowing and with flotsam on it, came the hooting of gibbons and a strange singing sound made by a symphony of countless insects.

I woke to see the river beneath my balcony and the mountain opposite veiled in cloud that eventually lifted to allow the sun in. A sign on the balcony rail asked me if I would like to climb this mountain. Surely they jest. It was vertical!

I could have stayed there happily forever but after five days I had to leave. On the outside wall of the boat landing office you put your name on a list if you wanted to travel on a particular day. Eight passengers were necessary to cover the cost of the boat to Luang Prabang. If less people wished to go they could make up the balance between them. There were seven names on my list so I trundled down to the landing with my transport, the wooden handcart that I had now become blasé about walking beside.

Organising the boat became a fiasco. The six other folk were French. They argued with the boatman for three quarters of an hour about paying for the extra place, one dollar twenty each. These were not shoestring travellers but older folk who looked reasonably well-heeled. When it seemed as though they were about to cancel the boat and take the bus I said I would pay the difference. It was the boatman who then gave in. He said that was not fair and that we could have the boat at the lesser price. I slipped him an extra ten dollars later because that was the price for the boat. He should not be running at a loss. And I liked him; he made the others involved look horrible.

The boat was the no-frills variety. The seats were one narrow plank down each side of the boat. I was again grateful for my seventy-cent cushion. It would require surgery to remove this valuable item from me before I left Laos, I decided. The river ran between tall green mountains with a few scattered villages at its edge, the houses of which were wood and rattan.

Three hours into the journey the boatman, who told me that he had been a monk for five years and that's where he learned a little English, pulled the boat up onto a sandy beach. We walked up a path to a village where an old woman let us use her toilet. On the way back, my friend the ex-monk insisted that we visit the temple that the villagers seemed so proud of. It was a pretty little open pavilion with a tiled floor. The French stepped in with their shoes on. What else would you expect of such meanies?

26 Into the Golden Triangle

It was just on dusk when we landed at the very long flight of steps that led up to Luang Prabang. An older man who looked like he needed the money got the job of carting my bag up to the top and then we wheeled it together along the riverfront to the Sayo River guesthouse. This was a nice old colonial house with balconies that face the Mekong waterfront.

The next day I moved to a guesthouse a little way out of the town that some people I met had recommended. The Thongbay Guesthouse required a rollercoaster ride on a dreadful dirt track to reach it, but it occupied a lovely riverside setting on a side shoot of the Nam Ou River. Once more the rooms were self-contained wooden bungalows facing the river and screened from each other by greenery. The guesthouse provided transport to Luang Prabang, only a few minutes away, several times a day. It poured again that night and all the next morning. The monsoon had definitely arrived.

That night there was a full moon and from my balcony I could see the golden stupa atop Phousi, the sacred mountain, glowing like a beacon. From the temple that sat on a hilltop on the other side of the river I heard the booming of the temple drum.

The extensive rustic garden that the bungalows were set in was lovely, even though every morning I had to clear the odd leech from the bathroom which had been tacked onto the back of the bungalow and was partially outside. I had provided a meal for a leech before I realised that this was what had caused the semicircular bleeding mark on my foot. At least leech bites don't itch or hurt. Conversely I enjoyed the lizards and geckos that ran about the roof and verandah.

I had come to Luang Prabang so that I could leave Laos at Houei Xai, the far northern border crossing to Thailand. I wanted to travel the mighty Mekong, 'the mother of waters' to the Lao, which has been venerated and worshipped for thousands of years. It is possible to travel all the way there from Luang Prabang by boat in two days with an overnight stop at Pak Beng. Boats do not travel the Mekong at night – there are too many hazards.

Having heard only bad reports about the regular boats, I set out to find the better one that I had read several accounts of on the internet as well as in the guide book. It proved impossible. All the travel shops that sold boat tickets in Luang Prabang denied it existed. Wherever I enquired, knowledge of a superior boat was non-existent so I took the address that was in the guidebook and showed it to various people. Three gave me directions; two drew maps of how to get there as did the staff at the Tourist Information Office. Later I discovered that the address they were all directing me to is actually in Thailand! No such street exists in Luang Prabang but I have three maps that show you how to get to it.

I gave up and was walking down the main street when I saw the office of an expensive but beautiful boat that does tours to the border and back. On the off chance that they might let me ride with them to Pak Beng where I wanted to stay for a couple of days, I went in. They fell on me with glad cries. Later I found that no one was booked on the boat for the trip up to the border but they had to go to collect a mob at the other end. I got a terrific deal – the ride and two nights at their super-swish Luang Say Lodge in Pak Beng. I would worry about how I continued on further when I got to Pak Beng but I had heard that the boats leaving from there were much better.

At the real dawn crack and not my regular dawn of nine am, a tuk tuk collected me and took me to the boat. Three more people had been dredged up, an Australian/Indonesian couple and a Lao man on a fact-finding expedition from another tour company – four people rattling around on this huge boat. Breakfast was served as the *Luang Say* got underway.

It took eleven hours to reach Pak Beng and the journey went past comfortable and fast approached luxury. The *Luang Say* was a purpose built thirty-four metre Mekong river barge. It had a well-stocked bar and a galley with a cook who did a great job – the food was terrific – and of course there was every traveller's priority, a five-star toilet. For the fourth time now I cruised up the Mekong as far as the junction of the Nam Ou River and the Caves of the Buddha, where we stopped for a visit, then continued following the Mekong north toward the Golden Triangle and Lao's border with Thailand and Burma.

The scenery was lovely, pristine green mountains or rocky karsts rising either side. We passed groups of people panning for gold on sandbanks or fishing. Few villages were visible from the water but the inevitable whisky village was located for our inspection. I began to wonder if the whole country was mad keen on getting pickled. The boat service, however, was remarkable after the roughing it I had done on regular boats. Cold towels and drinks were presented to us the minute we stepped back on board the boat.

The Luang Say Lodge was a short distance past Pak

Beng, which seen from the river as we went by looked to be just a straggle of mostly wooden, slightly ramshackle buildings climbing up the slope up a hill.

Female porters carted our bags up a long set of steps to the Lodge, which was quite the most wonderful place I have ever stayed. It was all wooden. Long walkways undulated through forests of plants and carefully kept gardens where colourful orchids cascaded from trees, to large bungalows with wood-shingled roofs. The reception and dining areas were on a covered deck overlooking the river. My bungalow had windows all around, a sitting area in front of the river, a great bathroom and a bed – a massive affair draped like the princess's bed in a fairy story with vast drifts of white netting. I felt I had stepped into a Somerset Maugham novel.

At seven the next morning I watched the *Luang Say* leave to continue its journey on to Houei Xai and after breakfast I set off to walk to the town. 'The road is dirty', the manager said on my way out. 'No worries', I replied 'what's a bit of dirt?' What she had omitted to say about the 'dirt', however, was that it was knee-high and mud. And that at times it stretched across the entire track. She also forgot to mention the steep hills and the landslides with tiny slippery mud paths around the edges of great drops. At one of these a village woman came up behind me, took my arm and steered me along it. I returned in a tuk tuk, which proved to be almost as interesting. But the view I had down to the river and the forest all around me as I walked along was spectacular and worth the effort. I had got up close and personal with the countryside.

Pak Beng is really just a big village. I wandered the length of the dirt main road passing the market's collection of shacks and stalls, a few simple shops and several guest-houses. At the boat office I bought a fifteen-dollar ticket for the next day's boat to Houei Xai.

That night as I sat in the dining area of the Lodge a French couple arrived fresh off the regular boat from Luang Prabang. The girl sat down at a table, put her head on her arms and began to sob loudly. I spoke to her and gave her a little pat or two but she didn't look up. She just kept on sobbing. The boat, I learned later, had been the last straw. As I keep saying, it's hard work being a tourist. Sometimes it all just gets to be too much. 'Have a good cry', I said 'it often helps'.

The next morning I convinced this nice young couple to take the next boat onwards with me. They had said that they'd had enough of boats and were going to bus it. This is not recommended – the road was said to be abysmal. Later the girl told me how nice it had been the night before to hear a kind voice even though she didn't see who it was. I suppose it helps that someone cares about your distress.

Fortunately I did not blot my good record by getting her onto a bad boat again. The boats travelling north from Pak Beng were not the same as those from Luang Prabang. This boat had soft seats and a toilet and room to walk down the middle – even drinks and munchies.

It took ten hours to reach Houei Xai but only because we were the local bus! We stopped for canoes that paddled up to us to transfer passengers, and at landings and places where there was no landing, only a canoe tied up to the bank. We took aboard lots of Lao who lay about the back section of the boat on sleeping mats when the seats ran out. There were more villages on this part of the river but there were no roads to them – their only access was the river.

So this was the infamous Golden Triangle, opium country. It looked pretty harmless to me. Opium growing was only outlawed by the government in the last decade and is not eliminated yet. Attempts to introduce alternative crops continue and entire tribal villages have been relocated from the hills where they traditionally grew opium as their main cash crop.

In places the river cut through deep gorges of solid rock and huge boulders jutted out of the water in the middle of the river. The mountain slopes were mostly jungle covered but some less high had rounded areas that had been cleared for crops or logging.

Houei Xai's waterfront was busy. Small ferries wove to and fro between the banks of Thailand and Laos and a barge pulled China Shipping containers. It was a muddy rocky scramble to get ashore to where a narrow strip of asphalt ran up a small lane that led to the main street of the town. I tuk tuked to the hotel that the guide book stated was the nicest in town. And that's definitely the last time I believe anything those blokes write. The 'nicest hotel in town' did not impress me. So, in the rain, I trundled my bag across the road and booked into the Mekong Hotel which was fine. I had a room at the rear of the building with a terrific view of the river and across it Thailand – heavily wooded hills, a few houses and a temple.

I walked down to the town centre. A fifteen minute walk they said. With jet propelled boots maybe. The town was small. It had a market, guesthouses, shops and one main street that wasn't very main – dogs slept in it, cars just manoeuvering around them.

At the restaurant attached to the Mekong I tried for dinner. They had no idea what I wanted and failed to understand I needed food. What did they think I was sitting there at dinnertime, clutching a knife and fork hopefully, for? I eventually got fed but I went down to the town for breakfast.

In a shop in the main street I bought a bus ticket that would take me from Houei Xai all the way to Chiang Mai in Thailand, from where I planned to take the train to

Bangkok. On the morning of departure I was taken from the shop in the main street on foot to the Lao Immigration checkpoint a few yards away down the lane that leads up from the boat landing. Then I clambered into a motorised canoe and was ferried across the river to Thailand, where I was put into a tuk tuk and taken to a guesthouse to wait for the bus. It turned out to be a minibus with only six passengers and was very comfortable.

It took five hours to reach Chiang Mai. The country was immediately different. It was more built up and there was more agriculture – rice and corn interspersed patches of forest. Chiang Mai seemed huge after the quiet of Laos.

The next morning I bought a ticket for the night train to Bangkok, arriving in the now-familiar Bangkok railway station. Deadbeat, I taxied to the White Orchid Hotel close to the station and fell into a bed. I was given a superior room at the front of the building with a large expanse of window and a raft of mod cons. I was happy. I suspect that the pleasure in travelling for me has become managing to be comfortable somewhere else. No more dossing down in sleazy two-dollar Singapore brothels. Been there. Done that. Over it.

Time to go home.

BEHIND THE VEIL
Lydia Laube

Cardiac resuscitation was often applied to a patient who was fast asleep. The hapless victim woke from a peaceful slumber to find somebody, often an infidel, jumping up and down on his chest.

Lydia Laube worked as a nurse in Saudi Arabia in a society that does not allow women to drive, vote, or speak to a man alone.

Wearing head-to-toe coverings in stifling heat, and battling administrative apathy, Lydia Laube kept her sanity and got her passport back.

Behind the Veil is the hilarious account of an Australian woman's battle against the odds. It will keep you entertained for hours.

ISBN 978 1 86254 267 9

For more information visit www.wakefieldpress.com.au

BOUND FOR VIETNAM
Lydia Laube

A chance conversation on the Trans Siberian Express en route
to Outer Mongolia causes Lydia Laube to veer off course and
take a long way home. She heads south thousands of kilometres to the eerie mountains of South China, in search of a
broachable pass into Vietnam.

Lydia never takes no for an answer. Against all protests she
finds ways to venture through rarely travelled parts of China,
overcoming language barriers and standing her ground in
crowded buses, boats and trains. She makes a meal of a snake
and submits to the ministrations of the Dental Department of
your worst nightmare.

Leaving China by pedal-power, Lydia enters Vietnam by
motorbike and discovers a beautiful and resilient country.

Sit tight as you ride with our brave lone traveller. Her
adventures will amaze and impress you.

ISBN 978 1 86254 462 8

For more information visit www.wakefieldpress.com.au

IS THIS THE WAY TO MADAGASCAR?
Lydia Laube

In all her travels across the globe, Lydia Laube had always
wanted to visit the intriguing island of Madagascar and meet
its famous residents, the lemurs. So she hops aboard a French
cargo ship, replete with cleaver-wielding cook, to begin a
wayward journey.

After escapades in Singapore, Egypt, Malta and Italy, Lydia
eventually lands on the place Arab sailors called the Island of
the Moon. Here she makes friends with the locals, attempts
to familiarise herself with their tricky language, and sets off to
sample the country's food, accommodation, sights, and sounds –
and to find her lemurs.

ISBN 978 1 86254 755 1

For more information visit www.wakefieldpress.com.au

LLAMA FOR LUNCH
Lydia Laube

Lydia Laube, one of the world's dauntless, intrepid travellers, is off to South America in search of the sun.

Braving hair-raising mountainous tracks, bandits, immigration officials, jungle beasts and third-world dentists, she ventures across Mexico, through the Panama Canal, along the coast of Colombia, and into Peru, Bolivia and Brazil. Lydia explores the last hideaway of the Incas, Machu Picchu, and, fulfilling a lifelong dream, sails down the mighty Amazon to the Atlantic.

She travels alone into regions that armies of men would dare not enter – and, eventually, she learns how to catch the right bus.

ISBN 978 1 86254 576 2

For more information visit www.wakefieldpress.com.au

SLOW BOAT TO MONGOLIA
Lydia Laube

Who else but Lydia Laube would climb the Great Wall of China waving a pink parasol while riding a donkey? In *Slow Boat to Mongolia* Lydia tells of her travels by ship, train and bone-shaking bus through Indonesia and China on her way to fabled Outer Mongolia.

Lydia learns to use chopsticks with aplomb and ploughs her way through crowds to visit places few westerners have ever seen. She reaches Outer Mongolia, where she stays in a *ger* in the snow and rides a horse through waist-high silvery grass.

ISBN 978 1 86254 418 5

For more information visit www.wakefieldpress.com.au

TEMPLES AND TUK TUKS
Travels in Cambodia
Lydia Laube

Lydia Laube discovers that Cambodia, a nation with a violent and horrific recent past, is also an ancient, beautiful country populated by friendly, generous people who like to ride motor-bikes very fast around corners.

Preferring the more sedate pace of tuk tuks, Lydia chooses this mode of transport wherever she can while visiting Cambodia's magnificent temples, markets, beaches and mountains – and, of course, the killing fields.

Deciphering the menu is only part of the intrigue of this mysterious land only just now opening to tourists and travellers. Join Lydia, squashed into a taxi with nine or so others, for an unforgettable ride.

ISBN 978 1 86254 631 8

For more information visit www.wakefieldpress.com.au

THE LONG WAY HOME
Nobody Goes *That* Way
Lydia Laube

I sat in the windowless and windscreenless front seat of the truck receiving proposals of marriage: only three, I must admit, but then I was only there three quarters of an hour and wasn't looking my best.

Lydia Laube worked as a nurse in Saudi Arabia and described her tribulations and triumphs in the best-selling traveller's yarn *Behind the Veil*.

Lydia Laube returned to Saudi Arabia, collected her pay, then decided to take *The Long Way Home* via Egypt, Sudan, Kenya and India.

Our Good Little Woman is as eccentric and entertaining as ever . . . blithely she trots along, sunshade held aloft, while behind her ships sink, hotels explode, and wars erupt.

ISBN 978 1 86254 325 6

For more information visit www.wakefieldpress.com.au